SILICON COLLAR

an optimistic perspective on
humans, machines and jobs

VINNIE MIRCHANDANI

To Rita and Tommy

As you start your careers, may you find your own R2-D2 and C-3PO to help you change our worlds for the better.

Table of Contents

Preface

∿→

This book has been four years in the making.

In 2012, I wrote *The New Technology Elite,* which looked at the trend of "smart" products and services across a wide range of industries. The book started off at the annual Consumer Electronics Show in Las Vegas. I described booths of wide variety where Walgreens demoed its mobile app for pharmacy refills, Whirlpool showcased its Duet washer/dryers with various laundry apps, and GM showed off an OnStar-equipped rearview mirror.

I asked in that book:

> "What's going on here? These companies live far from Silicon Valley and are known as retailers and auto companies. Why are they competing for booth space and geek attention with technology vendors?"

That book looked at how companies were rethinking their products and services from a new design lens, from a contract manufacturing vantage, and from an intellectual property protection perspective. While I looked at how these companies were marketing these new products and services, I did not look at how these products are being used by workers at home or deployed on the job to enhance the nature of their work.

This book brings that worker point of view to our attention. I examine how emerging technologies and machines—mobile apps, QR codes, drones, robots, artificial intelligence, autonomous vehicles, and exoskeletons among them—are reshaping jobs in every industry.

I profile over 50 jobs ranging from accountants to oilfield workers, to winemakers. These examples come from over 15 countries. Human beings and machines are joining forces in various permutations with the noble aim of making work safer, smarter, and speedier.

While the practitioners I interviewed were positive about the new technologies and their impact on work, a number of academicians, analysts, and economists are worried sick about the new machine age and envision a jobless future. Their pessimism, amplified by politicians, is leading to widespread gloom on the street. Internationally, it is even leading to referenda about whether citizens should be guaranteed minimum incomes, irrespective of work status, in anticipation of such jobless societies.

Why are so many smart people so pessimistic? Being a technology enthusiast for decades, I wondered what I might be missing. I found inspiration in something I had heard from Bill Joy, one of the cofounders of Sun Microsystems. Joy, who was once described by *Fortune* as the "Edison of the Internet," had this guidance: "If you cannot solve a problem, make the problem bigger. If you draw a bigger circle, you start to see several systems you can work on."

In the case of this book, drawing a bigger circle meant looking at how automation has gradually rolled out over the last century and not just in the last few years. For example, I researched the history of UPC codes and scanners with their impact on grocery jobs going all the way back to 1948. I researched how cars have gradually been taking over control of driving from humans since cruise control was first introduced to the masses by Chrysler in 1958. I similarly studied progress in artificial intelligence, robotics, and self-service technologies and their related impacts on jobs.

Then I made the circle even bigger. I studied how Japan, a voracious adopter of automation in the form of service robots, vending machines, and even conveyor-belt sushi, still keeps artisans working with skills that date back centuries.

This research gives me a confidence that we will continue to see "evolution, not revolution" when it comes to automation's impact on jobs today. Our societies have what I call "circuit breakers to overautomation." Machines will become more of our colleagues, and we should not be so worried about their increased presence in the future. If anything, they will take our outstanding workers and make them even better.

We should, instead, be worried about our fellow humans. I researched a number of man-made problems that have led to a dysfunctional labor economy. On the one hand, we have millions of unfilled jobs and, on the other hand, we have unhappy workers with trillions in student debt. My "circle" got even bigger upon analysis of the surprising "Brexit" vote for the UK to leave the EU. Exit polls show a significant number of older citizens voted to leave, whereas Millennials overwhelmingly wanted to remain. The aging U.S. worker is showing similar discontent, which the Presidential candidates have been tapping into.

I blended three perspectives for the book. As an innovation author, I catalogued the many jobs that are being transformed by technologies—from handsomely compensated basketball players to much less appreciated garbage collectors. Then I turned historian and looked at the impact of automation over decades. I found that we can expect a gradual impact on jobs to be the norm. Yes, as we have seen with farm jobs declining over the last century, we will get plenty of warning. I used that finding to confront the pessimism about jobless futures. Finally, putting on my analyst hat, I have looked at how employers, regulators, unions, and workers have all confused the labor economy.

The book is split into three parts.

Part I covers "machines as our colleagues" and how they help workers excel. It is covered in five chapters:

- Chapter 1 looks at jobs in Northern California, surrounding Silicon Valley: pro basketball players and coaches, animators, doctors and nurses, financial advisers, data center operators, R&D professionals, hospitality staff, and winemakers.

- Chapter 2 looks at jobs in less hospitable places, far from the Bay Area: in the oil patch, on the shop plant floor, in the military, in schools, in media, in commercial law, in the chemistry lab, and in urban planning.

- Chapter 3 looks at women and how with technology, they are reshaping various professions—in accounting, advertising, architecture, marketing, anthropology, and higher education.

- Chapter 4 looks at jobs in another Bay Area—the relatively low-tech Tampa Bay region: collecting garbage, delivering packages for UPS, roofing, making orange juice, running restaurants, working at Home Depot, driving for Uber, and shipping items from Amazon warehouses.

- Chapter 5, striking a contrast to the optimistic tones in the first four chapters, points out signs of discontent in the labor economy. These include younger workers with too much student debt, aging workers with too little to retire on, the backlash against globalization, and the mismatch in job vacancies and the supply of skill sets.

Part II focuses on our worries about "machines becoming our overlords":

- Chapter 6 presents the wide range of pessimistic voices sounding the alarm about jobless futures.

- Chapter 7 takes a historical look at how technology has been adopted gradually and analyzes its impact at the U.S. Post Office, in jobs driving vehicles, in public accounting, and at grocery stores.

- Chapter 8 covers a number of "braking mechanisms" which slow down adoption of automation, including technology hype cycles and incumbent interests.

- Chapter 9 looks at the promise of job gains, not just losses, from the next generations of technologies and related industries.

Part III focuses on what I call "guiltless automation":

- Chapter 10 analyzes in detail the many problems in today's labor economy and concludes that while we are worrying about machines, we should rather be focused on man-made problems.

- Chapter 11 has thoughts on how to approach automation and jobs—at societal, enterprise, and personal levels.

As usual, I have countless people to thank. Not just everyone who participated in the interviews and are in the pages that follow, but also those who made introductions to people I profiled. They include Marc Benioff, Nick Dembla, Susie Johnson, Howard Joyce, Rusty Sanborn, Frank Scavo, Julie Smith David, and others.

My book production team again did a stellar job. Mark Baven and my wife, Margaret Newman, share the editorial credit. Blending the three voices I described earlier was not easy. Michele and Ronda at 1106 Design once again did a superb job with the aesthetics. I am especially proud of their cover design.

These are confusing times. But one thing is for sure—whatever machines may do in the future, they cannot be blamed for today's messes.

Oscar Handlin, the 1952 Pulitzer Prize winner for history, opened his book *The Uprooted* with this: "Once I thought to write a history of the immigrants in America. Then I discovered that the immigrants were American history."[1]

I feel the same way. I planned to write a book about automation technology and its impact on workers. I discovered that the technology is nothing without outstanding workers.

So, I hope you find this an optimistic read on the changing nature of work, as well as a celebration of excellent workers and the technologies that are helping them excel.

---

[1]   https://www.amazon.com/Uprooted-Oscar-Handlin/dp/0316343137/ref=sr_1_ 1?s=books&ie=UTF8&qid=1467726052&sr=1-1&keywords=the+uprooted

The Allure of Machines

David Sugimoto, a third-generation Japanese-American, is an investment adviser. We went to school together, and you could always find him poring over stock prices and volume charts. We ran a small investment fund as part of our portfolio analysis class, and we would have endless debates about picking stocks using fundamental analysis versus his preferred charting and pattern-recognition approach. He could see trends in them that the rest of us could not. I was always curious how he got into finance since his family came from the manufacturing belt in Michigan, but I never pried. He recently shared with me his family history, and I was awestruck by the story of his maternal grandfather.

Tadae Shimoura came from a small village in Tokushima on the island of Shikoku, from a poor farming family. Somehow, even in the early 1900s, in that remote place, in the smallest of the four main Japanese islands, he became infatuated with the emerging automobile industry. Here was a young man who spoke no English and had no money to travel the 6,000+ miles to Detroit in a world where airplanes had still not been invented.

Said Sugimoto:

> "He somehow got a job on an English freighter as a fireman, shoveling coal into the furnace. The English freighter was a

means to learn English. He next got a job on an American freighter. Again, he was a fireman. When I was very young, I seem to recall he showed me a newspaper clipping about a ship which picked up survivors from the Titanic and said he had worked on that vessel.

One day his ship docked in New York City. He just got off the ship and did not return. Ethnic groups, as you know, tend to find their own communities. He found a boarding house with young Japanese men. One day the desk clerk asked him to mail some letters. My grandfather willingly took the stack and as he walked to post them, he flipped through the letters. He saw that one was addressed to a Japanese gentleman in Detroit. He made a note of that name, and eventually found his way to Detroit in 1912.

He looked this guy up and made his way to Edison Avenue. This Japanese man was the gardener of the grounds. My grandfather explained to the gardener he had come to Detroit to get a job in the automobile industry. The gardener said, 'Okay, let me go talk to my boss.' My grandfather asked, 'Who's he? Whose house is this anyway?' The gardener replied, 'You don't know who lives here? Well, this is Henry Ford's house.'

Henry Ford came out and told my grandfather to go to the Highland Park plant. You may have seen the famous picture where they turned out 1,000 Model Ts in a day. My grandfather became a rubber chemist for Ford Motor Co. That's how we ended up in Detroit and how my grandfather became the first Japanese national to work in the American automobile industry.

He met two other Japanese men in Detroit. One was named Sasakura and the other was Hirata. They became fast friends and decided to adopt American names—and they all decided on James.

During World War II, Ford geared up its Willow Run factory near Ypsilanti, Michigan, for B-24 Liberator bomber production. The government was uncomfortable with a Japanese immigrant at that plant. Edsel Ford supposedly told the government, 'If I can't have James Hirata working for me, you might as well shut down the plant.' At the Detroit Institute of Art, there is a sole Asian face among the workers depicted in a famous mural painted by the Mexican artist Diego Rivera. He's the only man who's wearing a white shirt and a tie. That is Hirata. He's memorialized in that picture.

James Sasakura went to work for Tucker Motor. He's been memorialized by Hollywood in the movie *Tucker,* by Francis Ford Coppola. His character is even identified in the movie as Jimmy. He eventually went on to work for the Ex-Cell-O Corporation and was the person who designed the machinery that forms and seals the wax-coated milk cartons.

My family can boast three generations in the car business. My father's first job was at Ethyl, a spinoff from GM, and my sister also went to work for GM. That's quite a tribute to the three Jimmys."

How inspirational is James Tadae Shimoura's story? A new machine, the automobile, made a young man travel against all odds halfway across the world. He would be fascinated to see his grandson using a very different type of technology in his investment career. (Eight of the 10 top hedge funds today are "quants"—they rely exclusively on computer models to tell them when and what to buy and sell.)

Are we any different today as we line up for blocks, waiting for the "Next New Thing"? What are young people around the world dreaming about, when it comes to today's new machines—drones, robots, thinking machines, and 3-D printers? Just as robo-advisers are rapidly changing Sugimoto's investment profession, what new careers await the coming generations, as we explore new frontiers in space travel, the deep seas, and medicine?

Machines as Colleagues

Chapter 1

Welcome to "Silicon Collar Valley"

⌁→

"I was alone and young and willful and unheeded, but I was happy and near to the wild heart of life."[2]

If that reminds you of James Joyce, you are right, it is Larry Ellison's interpretation. Ellison, billionaire founder of Oracle, invoked Joyce in a commencement speech at USC. He was describing how his family was disappointed he had given up on medical studies in Chicago and had moved to Berkeley, CA when he was 21. He also described how his wife thought he was spending too much time in the Sierras and on the Pacific, and not enough on pursuing a software career. And yet, he was at peace with his choices.

More about Ellison later, but five decades later, it is clear he has done just fine, and numerous other young people have followed his footsteps to the Bay Area and made it the technology capital of the world. No surprise, then, that every job in the region has been reshaped by waves of technology. Let's start with the Golden State Warriors in Oakland, which borders Berkeley.

---

[2] https://www.youtube.com/watch?v=5DJaWWwITRM

The "Curry Flurry"

Decades from now, basketball fans will be citing stats from the Warriors' incredible 2016 season. It took a never-been-done-before comeback from a 3–1 deficit by the Cleveland Cavaliers in the seven-game Finals to put an asterisk next to the miraculous season enjoyed by the Warriors.

The NBA team scored a total of 1,077 regular season 3-pointers, powered by the "Splash Brothers," Stephen Curry and Klay Thompson, easily outstripping the previous high of 933 set by the Houston Rockets in 2015. The team had 73 wins—the most by any NBA team in the regular season, eclipsing a record set by the legendary 1996 Chicago Bulls. While that record took 20 years to break, point guard Curry broke his own record for 286 3-pointers set in 2015. He blew past it to hit an unfathomable 402. In those two years, Curry scored more 3-pointers than the great Michael Jordan did over a 15-year period. Curry had a 45% 3-point shooting average in 2016, almost double the league average of 24%. He was the first-ever unanimously selected league MVP—getting all 131 first-place votes. At 6'3", Curry would have been considered undersized a few years ago; now he is representative of what NBA analysts say is becoming a game of "space and pace" where agility trumps player size.

Diehard fans can cite many more stats. But even they have access to only a tiny fraction of the data available to Warriors coaches and players. For Kirk Lacob, Assistant General Manager of the team, part of his job is to scout and introduce technologies infused with rich data to help make his players more competitive. It's a version of automation in the sports world. It's also leading to jokes as to whether Curry is a 3-point shooting robot.

In an interview, Lacob told me, "The reality is that we can't influence results completely—and we are a results business. But if we can push and pull the probabilities, we can hope to have a better outcome." That's a pretty modest statement about a team which won the 2015 NBA championship and almost repeated that achievement in 2016.

In order to tweak those probabilities, NBA teams have access to data from SportVU, a camera system hung from the rafters in sports arenas that collects data on everything throughout a game in x, y, and z planes. Lacob observed:

> "What's cool is that it allows us to follow everything that's going on in a game, whether we can see it or not. It's coordinate-based so you are using hard numbers, and we have some pretty talented software engineers and mathematicians to help us figure out exactly what it means to move from a specific coordinate to another. With 24 frames in a single second, you end up with about 1.3 million rows in a CSV file and with that we have truly quantified the game of basketball. It was originally an Israeli missile tracking technology that was retrofitted to track a basketball.
>
> Basketball is so much more difficult to track than, say, baseball. Baseball is a flat dimensional grid with players in certain areas and there's a pitch and a swing and it either makes contact or it doesn't. If you make contact, it goes to a specific place and is easy to grid. Basketball's never been easy to grid because of the difference in player sizes and speeds in a dynamically flowing game. SportVU has allowed us to quantify all of those movements. It doesn't mean that we figured the game out, but it has given us a deeper glance into what's going on."

The vast amount of data being collected is not just useful to the teams. It is also leading to smarter fans, as tools such as DataFX display analytics on Jumbotrons throughout games. Fan interest in sports metrics has skyrocketed in the last decade, with ESPN airing shows like *Numbers Don't Lie* and the network's magazine producing an annual analytics issue.

Lacob continued:

"Over the last three years, we've also been using various sensors and hardware in practice. Currently, we have GPS harnesses and heart rate monitors that players wear during practice. When you combine this with game data, which is motion-capture, you're able to get an even better understanding of what exactly is going on with the player's body throughout the year. The stronger your baselines are, the stronger the correlation is going to be with the in-game play. You are able to start to infer how healthy a player really is, how tired he is getting, when he needs a break, when he can push it to the edge of what he can do. This is only going to get better and better as it applies to the real world and biomedical science.

One technology we've looked at tracks muscle activity using an EKG reading directly from sensors on the body. It's made by a start-up called Athos which produces compression, sweat-wicking fabric with trackers that send information via Bluetooth to mobile devices. The clothing can monitor electromyography, measure muscle activity, heart rate, and other metrics.

They figured out a way to do that wirelessly so it's noninvasive. This should hopefully give us a much more accurate reading of what's going on with the player's body. Our goal is to eventually look at a fatigue bar, like in a video game, and observe, 'You know, his left quad is firing at 70%. Well, with our baseline, he should be firing at 80% at this point of the game. Something may be wrong. Let's get him out of there.' It doesn't mean he's necessarily hurt, but he could be on the way to getting hurt. Sometimes it could be an injury that we haven't yet sniffed out. This is all about allowing us to have more information, to make better decisions and increase our probabilities.

I have just talked about predictive injury analytics. You'd rather a player not get hurt than have to heal him back to health, but the reality is that injuries happen. Since we've taken a baseline reading on all of these different instruments, we're able to use that as a 'return to play' guidance. Players usually tell you they feel great. You can watch them and go, 'Their gait looks fine. They don't look like they drag at all,' but if you go to the read, you can find, 'You know what? They're just a step off,' or 'The muscle reading is telling us that he's actually not quite there yet. He's at 90%.' The reality is we need a guy at 95% before he's really deemed back to playing standards. All these things can be used to decide on a return to play, as well as predictive injury prevention."

Next, he discussed Keemotion:

"It's a single-camera unit set up in our practice facility, as well as our D-league facility in Santa Cruz. It allows us to film practice in real time and do real time cut-ups. This way we don't need somebody staying up with a camcorder, following the play, and then going and afterward cutting up film. I'm able to watch practice from wherever I am situated. I can have a whole cut-up of a 90 minute practice compressed into 20 minutes, if I want it, the moment it's over. That has really changed scouting and the practice side of things for the better and has given us a whole new lens through which to see our world."

How do players and coaches react to all this automation?

"You have some players who are very interested because they're looking to prolong their career or they're looking to find an edge. For other players, it's just too much. Our attitude is, 'If you want more information, we'll give you the information.' We're not going to hold it back from a player or a coach, but if they don't want it—and we can tell, because we have people who deal with them every day and know what makes each player and coach tick—then we're not going to force it on them. Absolutely not going to."

The technology that the Warriors are experimenting with will similarly show up around the NBA. Venture capitalists and other technology executives—including Lacob's father, Joe Lacob, a partner at Kleiner Perkins; Steve Ballmer, ex-CEO of Microsoft; and Mark Cuban, founder and investor of many tech companies— have acquired majority interests in roughly half of the NBA teams.

Such technology will next filter down to college and high school basketball. *BusinessWeek* had a profile of another technology, from Noah Basketball, that the Warriors are trying out: "Noah uses the same sensor that powers Microsoft's Xbox Kinect. It's mounted about 13 feet above the rim and captures the position of the ball 30 times per second. The speaker can be set to call out the shot's angle, depth, or how far off center it was, left or right."[3] John Carter, Noah's CEO, is quoted: "Only 1 out of 11 high school players are shooting the right arc and depth. At the college level, that number climbs to about 50%. At the NBA level, it's probably 85%."

The technology will also spread around the world as Serbia, Brazil, Nigeria, and many other countries seek an advantage in the sport.

When a history of basketball is written a few decades from now, it will recognize this decade as one when technology and data transformed the sport. In a sign of the times, Lacob has been named to *Forbes'* "30 Under 30" Sports List along with world-class athletes like Usain Bolt and LeBron James. And Curry will inspire a new generation of players. NBA Commissioner Adam Silver has said in reference to Curry being undersized: "You can't dream of

---

[3] http://www.bloomberg.com/news/articles/2016-06-08/this-robot-knows-shooting-better-than-steph-curry

being 7-feet tall, but you can work and become a fantastic competitor on the floor."[4]

Animation Magic

In Emeryville, not far from Oakland, is a company that has reshaped another form of entertainment and modernized thousands of jobs. Blessed with the influence of George Lucas of *Star Wars* fame and Steve Jobs of Apple (who invested in Pixar), and geniuses like John Lasseter and Ed Catmull (who, fittingly, has written a book called *Creativity, Inc.*), Pixar was always destined to be a major influence in the film world.

Pixar, in its early incarnation, made short films and commercials, while advancing the state of the film industry with a focus on digital (nonlinear) film and sound editing. The company took off with *Toy Story*, a huge commercial success in 1995, and has since gone from one blockbuster success to the next.

In doing so, it has encouraged competitors like DreamWorks and Walt Disney Animation Studios while also reinvigorating the animation genre. (Disney now owns Pixar, but to keep the creative juices going, the animation groups are kept competitive.)

The movies appeal to a wide swath of audience. Grown-ups chuckle at the sequence in *Zootopia*, the recent Disney production where all workers at the DMV—the Department of Mammal Vehicles—are three-toed sloths. They are painfully slow at work but drive incredibly fast on the road.

Time wrote:

> "Just as a cigar is never really just a cigar, a Pixar movie is never really just a Pixar movie. Grownups delight in pointing out that these painstakingly crafted entertainments are always, deep down, about important things: the inner

---

[4] http://www.sfchronicle.com/warriors/article/Commissioner-Adam-Silver-in-favor-of-Warriors-7960811.php

life of preteen girls, the need for family and community, the recognition that it's O.K. to be different or to feel overwhelmed by everyday life. Meanwhile, kids just come for the talking fish."[5]

Even if you are not a fan of animated movies, it can be educational to spend a few minutes watching the credits at the end of *Zootopia*. Watch the names roll by listing hundreds of animators, sound-effect technicians, and stereoscopic artists who helped create the movie's 64 different animal species. There are 800,000 character models (baby, mama, grandpa, etc. of each species) in the movie. For each character, they created individual hair—the giraffe alone has nine million individual hairs! To do this takes gobs of computing power, with some frames taking up to 100 hours to render. However, even in these days of computer-generated imagery, the credits point to the immense talent which brings the characters to life.

These are modern day descendants of the Disney artists who, in 1937, created the first fully animated feature film, *Snow White and the Seven Dwarfs*. The Xerox copying process had just been invented. The xerography machine in a dedicated room with conveyor belts had been the critical technology for many other animation classics that followed *Snow White*.

Animation is an even bigger phenomenon in countries like Japan, where *manga* has traditionally attracted adult audiences and not just children. Korean animators have benefited from outsourcing from Japan and the U.S. and have blossomed on their own. China is also becoming a major player with firms like Wanda Group, which is building a $9 billion film studio and theme park complex. The Oriental-DreamWorks joint venture showed off the collaboration between Chinese and U.S. animators in the recent hit, *Kung Fu Panda 3*. Pixar's influence is also visible in these countries with software like RenderMan, which today is the industry

---

[5]   http://time.com/4371173/finding-dory-review/

standard for rendering computer graphics in film. Such technology keeps evolving. For *Zootopia*'s millions of animal hairs, the Disney team customized a fur shader to mirror how light would reflect off different strands, and applied ambient movement to reflect how wind moves those strands.

It's almost de rigueur these days for animated movies to be also shot in 3-D. In the next wave, virtual reality headsets like the Oculus Rift will allow for even more "immersive" experiences. Industrial Light & Magic, a unit of Lucasfilm Ltd. in San Francisco, has an Experience Lab whose goal is to "develop virtual reality, augmented reality, real-time cinema, theme park entertainment, and narrative-based experiences for future platforms." The lab is creating a new generation of tech-savvy workers for the entertainment industry.

Beyond the many digital jobs in Hollywood and Asia, animation has contributed to jobs at theaters which now boast 3-D viewing and Dolby sound technologies. It has led to massive new distribution channels in the form of Netflix/Amazon streaming and sales of Blu-Ray discs.

The animated characters have led to a ripple effect of creating new jobs at toy makers like Mattel and Hasbro which manufacture Disney and other popular merchandise. The animated characters have also led to growth in jobs at amusement parks where their human replicas are hugely popular. These days, the Anna and Elsa characters from the movie *Frozen* are as popular at Disney World as perennial favorites like Mickey Mouse. Epcot Center now offers a cool new ride, *Frozen Ever After*.

Digital Health Care

Across the Bay is the University of California, San Francisco (UCSF) Medical Center, a research and teaching hospital. In an interview, Dr. Michael Blum, the hospital's Chief Medical Information Officer, discussed its Center for Digital Health Innovation, which is an incubator for research projects like Health eHeart, a clinical trials platform using social media, mobile technology, and real-time sensors to revolutionize the treatment of heart disease.

Blum described a wide swath of cutting-edge technologies that help his doctors, nurses, and patients:

> "Our industry had over 100 years of activity being recorded on paper with analog data collection. That has prompted us to a digital transition. It's been slower in our industry because there were very few business drivers to really force this automation. A couple of early leaders such as Kaiser and Geisinger have been pioneering the transition. The tipping point came when the federal government passed the HITECH Act in 2009. I estimate that has taken us from 5% of electronic documentation in ambulatory practices up into the 80% range; and hospital-based electronic health records going from the 15%–20% range into the 90%–95%.
>
> That was a seminal transition for the industry, but unfortunately we went through that transition with dated technology. We ended up putting in a huge amount of technology at a very large cost that is arguably not well-positioned to support the future of where health care is going. That's led to a lot of the popular press and analysts saying that automation in health care has been a failure, when, in fact, I would say we're in the midst of a productivity paradox caused by a first pass at automation.
>
> Over the next few years, we're going to transition into a series of much more effective tools, tools that are built with newer technologies and newer paradigms. They will support both the provision of care in a much more effective way and support patient engagement with health care in ways that we haven't seen previously. On the patient and consumer side, we are also seeing digital tools rapidly evolving with sensors, wearables, and apps that will allow us to create a much better patient engagement experience.

At the same time, we are seeing automation in genomic and metabolomic [scientific study of chemical processes involving metabolites] spaces that are going to dramatically change health care delivery and move us to precision medicine. Over the next decade, we will look back and call today the Dark Ages of data and information in health care.

Just by having electronic health records, we have seen significant benefits that don't get widely reported or celebrated. For instance, as part of our automation we put in a robotic pharmacy that's linked to our electronic health records. The machine bundles appropriate pills and ensures that exactly what was ordered ends up in a sealed, bar-coded package. Then a nurse can scan and deliver it to the right patient at the right time and in the right dosage. There's a whole other story in the move from just hanging IV drips, where nurses would estimate and use mechanically alarmed devices to establish the flow rate in the drug administration. We now have automated infusion pumps. Eventually, we will get to the point where the pump can be programmed and controlled directly from the health record so that the pump could be blocked from giving a dangerously high dose. Also, if there's an adjustment to the dose, it could be controlled without having to manually reprogram the pump.

We know that in the past you commonly had the wrong patient getting the wrong dose at the wrong time. With the robotic pharmacy and automated infusion pumps, we have significantly reduced such errors. Of course, it needs to be balanced with concerns that the FDA has highlighted about such devices and the need for appropriate controls to keep out bad actors.

A similar transition is happening with ventilators, which for a long time were controlled by a respiratory therapist or intensivist, turning dials on an analog machine. Those have, for the most part, transitioned to digital controls and once connected to the network should allow the device to be controlled from a dashboard within an automated setting."

Blum next discussed cognitive computing and its impact on health care:

"If you look at AI and machine learning around cancer treatments, they are scaling rapidly. The focus on genomics and proteomics [the study of proteins] is leading to a much more rapid discovery than has ever happened before, with progress in previously untreatable cancers or those that were incredibly difficult to manage. Matching genomics to appropriate targeted therapies was not doable five years ago. We are seeing rapid progression and drug development in those spaces, and in targeted therapies and immunotherapies. Cancer is an obvious space because it's relatively easy to look at specific mutations and match the somatic mutations to targeted therapies.

The next frontier is germline mutations and diseases that people are predisposed to, and how those evolve over their lives. This depends on their environmental exposures; their social, economic, and emotional factors, and their nutrition which can lead to chronic disease. This is the next frontier that's going to need a lot of the artificial intelligence, machine learning, deep learning, that you'll see playing out as a follow-up to the earlier success in the somatic mutation space."

Dr. Blum on robots in the hospital:

"During surgeries, robots can be positioned at angles which are impossible for humans. They can also make more precise incisions, which can lead to less blood loss and quicker patient recovery. It's different than robotic automation in manufacturing where it's mostly about reliability and repeatability. We get that from our TUG robots which carry supplies and our pharmacy robots where we have dramatically lowered errors."

Dr. Blum next talked about transcription:

"For decades, doctors would dictate their surgical notes, procedure notes, and discharge summaries. Armies of humans would then transcribe these notes into a digital document. Gradually, speech-to-text technology from companies like Nuance has now evolved to a 99% or better accuracy in well-implemented systems. The ability to train to a particular voice has gotten much better. The ability to recognize dialects and accents has gotten much, much better. Radiology is one of the best examples of its use because it has a somewhat constrained medical vocabulary. The question these days is whether to transcribe or transition to structured data and then have the records create a text document. It would actually be preferable to move to a space where we weren't just creating these long text notes but were instead creating usable, structured, granular data that the machine can work on. Having said that, we need a blend—it's hard to convey a patient's story in individual words and data elements. Speech-to-text isn't going to be the answer for everything, but neither is filling in forms and checking boxes."

Dr. Blum is especially proud of the automation in the Children's Hospital:

"It's a very large space that would normally require a lot of people walking around. We have TUG robots wandering throughout delivering supplies. There's technology to protect against child abductions and unauthorized visitors. There are also little things like the ability to order their meals from the interactive in-room system. We provide the children with electronic games, entertainment, and education from the same system. We have even brought the school to the hospital, so they can continue their learning. It's been a very forward-thinking space that's gotten to be a national showcase for the steps taken in the direction of using technology and also for patient engagement."

How do health care professionals view such automation? Dr. Blum summarized:

"There's a perception that doctors and nurses are technophobic and push back on computers and automation because they separate the providers from the patient. I think that's untrue. Yes, we are in a caring profession where we need to have a human bond with the patient to best care for them. However, we also appreciate tools that help us do our best for patients. The magic happens when we find technologies and automation that simply disappear—they help us provide better care for our patients without being in the way."

A Renaissance Man's Perspective

Whenever I visit the Bay area, especially when I start to write a new book, I like to talk to Ray Lane. Do a quick scan of his Wikipedia page and you see Executive Chairman at HP, Partner at Kleiner Perkins, President of Oracle, and Chairman of the Board of Trustees at Carnegie-Mellon University, among other entries. And beyond his achievements, he always has an interesting point of view on a wide array of topics.

For this book, I asked him to talk about his early career and to frame how those professions have evolved with advancing technology. He talked about his time at Booz Allen, the strategy consulting firm, and at EDS, the outsourcing firm.

Lane first talked about his time at Booz Allen in the 1980s:

"Booz was probably best known for its operations practice. They'd go in and do manufacturing and supply chain strategies. The guys that came out of that practice were black belts. They were really, really good. Our Cleveland office was the Mecca for operations management. If it was easy they thought it wasn't worth Booz doing it. It had to be hard and painful. I was brought in from EDS because they could see IT insights were becoming more and more important to formulating strategy. Remember, in the 1980s we were already talking about technology-enabled competitive advantage for American Airlines, McKesson, and others. I'd go into these strategy assignments with guys that were partner level, that came out of Harvard but knew nothing about IT. In reverse, I was learning stuff from them like how to do regression analysis that I would have learned if I had gone to business school. They would talk in language like "the R square coefficient is 81." [Lane is being modest—his college degree was in math and engineering.]

Of course, using today's lens, neither the client nor Booz was truly tech-savvy. Typically, half of a three-to-four month assignment would be spent collecting data. We would be digging through reports, through files, through computer systems that they had in those days, but it was largely manual. And from our side, when we went to crunch the data to report back to the client, it was all manual. I'll never forget—we actually used correcting tape. We would be up all night drafting a revision, and the corrections were made with pasted tape. You typed over it, took a copy, and it looked like it's an original revised version. If we wanted to show a graph of how something trended over time, we'd have an artist draw the graph on his drafting board, and then pull it into a report.

Then PCs arrived. Lotus 1-2-3 and Excel changed this business overnight, and it really was amazing. The artist, the drafting table, and the correcting tape were no longer needed, but the real value was that you could do analysis on the fly, and you could keep revising these reports way up until the time you had to go deliver them."

These days, clients supplement strategy consultants with internal analysts who can crunch massive data sets with Big Data tools like Hadoop, and can present them in impressive ways using visualization tools like Tableau.

The strategy firms of old (Booz, McKinsey, and others) have been joined by a new set of boutiques. Design firms like Ideo, digital agencies like Grok, and data-driven firms like Mu Sigma are hiring today's analysts. In a statement on the state of the market, ERP software vendor Infor, by no stretch a strategy consulting firm, has its own captive design agency, Hook+Loop, a design "garage," and Dynamic Science Labs with its own data wizards.

Lane next talked about his time at EDS, circa the 1970s:

"It used to be a great business, because clients didn't know how to run a data center. We'd call them oxen in a ditch— because they didn't know how to run. That was [founder] Ross Perot's belief: 'They don't have the IT skills; they don't know how to run their IT.' We would sign a five-to-eight year contract to manage their IT.

We would hire SEDs and OPDs. SEDs were system engineers that knew how to build and run systems and OPDs were the operators. They could run a data center better than anyone else."

Beyond the engineers and operators, there were plenty of other staff in EDS's 270-acre headquarters in Plano, TX, which was once the envy of many CIOs.

Lane made a telling point: "The world has changed. Most big companies today have the scale to run at the efficiency of EDS."

And "digital-native" companies like Google and Facebook dwarf the computing scale EDS had in the past. Additionally, they have considerably advanced the science of data centers. In my book *The New Technology Elite*, I profiled the Prineville, OR data center that Facebook opened in 2011: "Adding up all the efficiencies Facebook implemented in the data center, it says it delivered a 38% energy efficiency and a 24% lower cost compared to comparable existing facilities. The data center is rated at a power usage effectiveness (PUE) of 1.07—one of the best in the industry and much better than the 1.5 in its previous facilities."[6]

Even more impressive are the labor efficiencies of these data centers—less than 40 staff run that Facebook facility, which is spread over a 120-acre lot.

Companies like Amazon have turned such efficiencies into a very competitive product. On any given Sunday night, as Netflix subscribers watch their favorite shows, 30% of US web bandwidth runs through Amazon Web Services (AWS). Most corporate customers use AWS more sparingly but like its "pay as you go" model, compared to multiyear hosting contracts they had to sign until recently. Automation at AWS is accelerating. It features services like Lambda, which is described on its site:

> "AWS Lambda lets you run code without provisioning or managing servers. You pay only for the compute time you consume—there is no charge when your code is not running. With Lambda, you can run code for virtually any type of application or backend service—all with zero administration. Just upload your code and Lambda takes care of everything required to run and scale your code with high availability."[7]

---

[6]   https://www.amazon.com/New-Technology-Elite-Consumption-Production/dp/1118103130
[7]   https://aws.amazon.com/lambda/

EDS was acquired by HP in 2008. While HP tried to restore it to its former glory, its successor, HP Enterprise, eventually spun off the services business to CSC in 2016.

Recode wrote about the divestiture:

> "The new company—HPE and CSC are calling it Spinco for now—will be a pure player in the low-margin IT outsourcing market that had been a shrinking, expensive weight around the old HP's neck during the time it was struggling to bounce back. Revenue in the unit has declined for several years, during years that its customers went through wrenching changes in how they purchase and consume technology."[8]

Robo-Advisers

Nearby in San Francisco, we find the headquarters of Charles Schwab Corp. An upstart to big New York banks when it was founded in 1971, it is now part of the financial establishment, with $2.5 trillion under management. These days, it is Schwab that is being threatened by a new set of upstarts.

As *FastCompany* reported, "Companies such as Wealthfront, Betterment, and FutureAdvisor offer 'robo-adviser' services. Rather than investing money based on the decisions of a human expert, they use technology to manage a portfolio and recalibrate it on an ongoing basis. Doing so allows them to grind down fees, and poses a threat to the conventional business model of a company like Schwab, which is very much used to monetizing the wisdom of human beings."[9]

---

[8]   http://www.recode.net/2016/5/24/11763362/hpe-spins-off-services-deal-csc
[9]   http://www.fastcompany.com/3059565/how-charles-schwab-fought-back-against-the-robo-adviser-startups?utm_content=buffera2346&utm_medium=social&utm_source=twitter.com&utm_campaign=buffer

So Schwab has responded with its own Schwab Intelligent Portfolios, which it markets as "an online investment advisory service that builds, monitors, and rebalances your portfolio—so you don't have to."

Schwab describes the business model: "Other robo-adviser services carry low fees; Schwab one-ups them by not charging a fee at all for the service itself. Not that it's doing this out of the goodness of its heart: It makes money from the fees investors pay for individual exchange-traded funds, or ETFs, in their portfolios, and all portfolios include some cash managed by its Schwab Bank."

Schwab supplements the robo-service with a small team that can give financial planning guidance. As one executive told *Business Week*, "Finding that a lot of their clients value the human element was a little surprise for us. They trust the system but like to know that someone is verifying the information."[10]

While it's still tiny—the service has $6 billion under management and a team of 300 (out of a total staff of 15,000)—it positions Schwab to compete with the start-ups as the market gradually warms up to robo-advisers.

The R&D Lab Reimagined

Continuing southward in San Francisco, we can get a glimpse at automation in the R&D function.

Hampton Creek, which has funding from some of the most prominent investors in Silicon Valley, has been identified by Bill Gates as one of the companies shaping the future of food.

The start-up's initial focus was the global poultry industry—which lays two trillion eggs every year—but Hampton Creek is now looking at over 40 new foods, all of which are free of animal products.

---

[10] http://www.bloomberg.com/news/articles/2016-04-20/for-robo-advisers-the-next-bear-market-is-make-or-break

CEO Josh Tetrick told me:

> "We'll do north of $100 million in sales this year. About 50% of our sales are from food service to 3,300 public schools, nearly 500 universities and lots of corporate cafes. The other 50% are in retail, places like Target and Walmart and soon we'll be doing e-commerce. Given the nature of food service, we could serve a seven-year-old kid in a public school and then a 77-year-old retired person. In retail, our typical customer is a single mom . . . not that she is making an environmental statement; she just doesn't want to feed her kid crappy food."

His VP of R&D, Lee Chae, whose doctoral dissertation was on "Computational and Functional Genomic Analysis of the Receptor-Like Kinase Superfamily," explained:

> "We think about food as a system and it's a system made up of several ingredients. Each ingredient provides one or more functionalities. We look at them from an outsider's point of view—do any of those ingredients not make sense?
>
> I'll give you an example with our Just Mayo product. To make traditional mayonnaise you have to farm chickens. You grow grain, harvest the grain, feed it to the chickens. The chicken lays an egg, you break the egg, you separate out the egg white from the egg yolk. You take the yolk, you add oil, you whip it, and it turns into mayonnaise. That egg yolk, that is the ingredient providing the main key functionality in mayonnaise and it binds the oil.
>
> What if we were to grow grain, extract out a protein that has the same functionality of binding the oil and turn it into mayo. You save all those steps. People don't buy mayo because they want to eat eggs. They buy mayo because they want to eat mayo. In our thinking, egg's just a senseless

ingredient. By doing it our way, we just cut out all those steps. We saved on land, water, and energy.

With that conception of how we think about food, what we do on the R&D end is investigate and search the plant kingdom for proteins that are functionality related to food. We source produce from around the world. We bring them in, we do raw materials processing on them using all natural solutions and forces, to size-reduce the material and get it into an aqueous solution. We fraction it out into different protein samples and then we examine each of those fractions for basic molecular and biochemical properties just to understand the fundamental nature of that protein. Then we test it for functionality related to food. A lot of the food chemistry that we assay for, is for surface chemistry, water chemistry, structural interaction, etc.

Based on this research, we can create models that tell us that for this kind of food system, this kind of function, you should be looking at these types of proteins, with these types of characteristics, in these types of plants. In the plant landscape, there's at least 20 billion different types of proteins. So, you need a way to search that space efficiently. We are part of the food tech movement, but I say our technology is really a search technology."

Tetrick, discussing the company's initial Just Mayo product, noted:

"Our goal is to take the animal entirely out of the equation. We want to replace the egg-laying hen in these cramped, filthy conditions with plants that do exactly the same thing as her egg does. That could be to bind a cookie, make a muffin rise, or hold oil or water together in mayonnaise. Soon, we will also have plant-based scrambled eggs."[11]

---

[11] http://responsibleeatingandliving.com/favorites/josh-tetrick-beyond-eggs/

Forbes wrote about him:

> "Tetrick, a former Fulbright fellow, says his drive to remake the food system grew from his experiences in Africa, where he spent seven years working on projects related to poverty, farming and malnutrition. He's also motivated by his own sense of mortality. While he was in law school, Tetrick was diagnosed with hypertrophic cardiomyopathy, a heart condition that he says makes him more appreciative of 'life's fragility.' A message flashes every morning on his phone: 'Prepare to die today.'"[12]

Chae said:

> "What's interesting is that we are not taking an existing process that is already been established in industry and then automating it. We created a new methodology and process by hand, validated it and gave it the proof of principle. We can show products on a shelf and demonstrate that our research approach works. Now we are scaling up to do this with automation. It's a whole new process that was prototyped by scientists doing it manually. It's quite different from having an existing workforce for a while, that you later automate."

How is that changing the nature of the R&D lab job? Tetrick explained:

> "We're screening through about 400,000 species of plants in the course of the next couple of years. That would be tough if you're just using the human hand and just the human brain. So, we're investing all these tens of millions of dollars in automation. Our scientists are not staying up all night. The

---

12 http://www.forbes.com/sites/robindschatz/2016/04/30/hampton-creek-ceo-josh-tetrick-talks-about-the-challenges-of-scaling-fast-interview/#322667b3173e

machines are up and running assays. As this data is being generated, hypotheses are being populated into the cloud, and then we can make smart decisions when we actually wake up and analyze the data.

We have a number of plant biologists, molecular biologists and biochemists. We have material scientists, food scientists, and we have automation engineers. We have process engineers, including certification people, and we have our data scientists and computational biologists. No offense to Kraft, General Mills, or Nestle, but I am not sure they could say the same thing about the staff mix in their R&D."

Hotel California

Let's head a little bit due south, next to all the venture capitalists in Menlo Park. There, Avi Haksar is the managing director of the lush, expensive 16 acres of real estate that constitute the Rosewood Sand Hill resort. After studying at Les Roches International School of Hotel Management in Switzerland, Haksar has spent a long career in high-end hospitality, including the Four Seasons and other Rosewood hotels around the world.

He discussed with me how technology is reshaping work in his industry:

"Rosewood is in the top end of the luxury hospitality market. Our guests are select business people and high-end clientele. They have the same expectations wherever they go. The same guest who visits us here also travels to New York and Dallas for business. Their expectations of 'high touch' service are consistent, and different from those of someone who stays overnight at, say, a midpriced business hotel.

Still, the technology-driven changes are remarkable. In the old days, hospitality meant human interaction in the form of meeting and greeting at the check-in counter. Today, the guests are not standing at the front desk wasting time.

Or think of the booking process in the past. You would call the hotel. There would be a person on the other end of the phone who would talk to you, explain the product and all the amenities. Today, our guests don't have to make time for that phone call when they can book via the web. In some hotels the check-in process is completely automated—via your mobile phone or by kiosk.

In the luxury hospitality segment we are still striving for that conversation with the guest. We are moving to handheld devices—we call them 'rovers'—where we can check them in while we walk them to their bungalow. The personal interaction continues but it is much more efficient for the guest.

There are plenty of other areas where the guest does *not* want the interaction with one of our staff, and there you see even more impact on the industry. Guests expect to have iPhone and Samsung chargers available in the room. They want easily accessible plugs, so room designs have changed. They don't want to pick up the phone and talk to room service when they can order online. They don't want paper magazines. They want to read digital versions or stream Netflix and other services directly on the room TV. Minibars: in the past, someone would come to your room to inventory and account for your usage. With sensors today, we have automated that task. We used to have the really big, old, clunky, brass room key and that evolved to plastic cards. Now, there are keys on mobile phones. Restaurant reservations—most guests just go to OpenTable. In the future, we could see more robotic room cleaning—again, in areas where the guest does not need interaction with our staff.

Should there be robotic butlers or robotic bartenders that are found at the big casinos in Vegas? Or highly automated kitchens? Or the electronic drapes that you see in Asian hotels? That is our big deciding factor about automation—does the guest want the human touch or have a machine provide a service? I am not sure our guests want too much of that personal interaction or chef ingenuity to go away."

While Haksar wants to keep the "high-touch" service at his hotel, within a few miles there are visible signs of the technology that hospitality workers are adjusting to, at the midpriced business hotels he mentioned.

For example, the Hyatt Regency, near the San Francisco airport, has at its car rental counter a NCR-developed Hertz ExpressRent kiosk. It enables video-chat access to a live agent for after-hours transactions and for assistance in multiple languages. The kiosk can also scan your driver's license and print your contract. The hotel has cards with QR codes you can scan with your mobile phone to show nearby jogging trails. No need to bother the concierge for that piece of information. One of those trails runs parallel to the airport's Runway 28L, and you can try and keep up with the constant traffic of Boeing 747s and Airbus A380s.

A Marriott hotel, on that jogging trail, has large displays which show live traffic information on nearby roads, including the perennially busy Highway 101. The hotel has a lounge with a self-serve espresso machine and automated wine dispenser. You can check in to your room a day in advance with the chain's mobile app, and when you show up pick up your key card.

The Starwood Aloft hotel, near Apple's headquarters in Cupertino, has robotic butlers. When a guest needs extra towels, a "Botlr" delivers them. Sensors and wireless connectivity allows it to communicate with the hotel and the elevator software, enabling it to navigate the hotel without running into people or objects.

Hotel Diva in downtown San Francisco does away with the key card. The Mobile Key app allows you to open your room with your smartphone. The Marriott Marquis nearby has tablets in every room, and allows guests to access Yelp's Eat24 which showcases a wide range of dining that can be delivered to your room.

White Collar Bots

Continuing further south, in San Jose, we encounter Mihir Shukla, CEO of Automation Anywhere. He has a modest ambition aimed at using business process bots that perform task-based work alongside humans, freeing the human employee to focus on higher value work:

> "You know Uber is the world's largest taxi company but doesn't own taxis. And Airbnb is the largest hospitality company but doesn't own real estate. We want to be the world's largest employer with the fewest number of people."

He imagines this to be the workforce of the future for the modern enterprise—human workers (FTEs, or full-time employees) working alongside software robots (AFTEs, or automated full-time equivalents). "We've automated over two million hours of manual work," said Shukla. "And this is just the beginning."

Shukla is delivering this solution today in a category called Robotic Process Automation (RPA)—process bots for a wide range of knowledge worker jobs: the help desk and other positions. An example comes from ANZ Bank, which has deployed hundreds of business process bots that join human FTEs in handling low-level tasks in its institutional and retail banking businesses. By the end of 2016, they expect to have more than 1,200 bots up and running in their digital workforce. These bots help with processes such as progress payments for construction loan mortgages and audit certificates that integrate data from several ANZ systems. Shukla said the best marketing of the ANZ back office has been to say to its business units: "Bring as much business as you want us to process. We are not a bottleneck anymore."

The FTEs, many of whom are highly qualified, have embraced bots doing much of the tactical, task-based work. Shukla says most of Automation Anywhere's customers are not using bots to replace employees but to supplement them for future growth.

He cites the example of a 200,000-employee company which may need to grow to a head count of 350,000. It will likely hire 50,000 people, but supplement them with 100,000 bots.

And this is not just for banking. Another global customer is AT&T, headquartered in Dallas. In the earlier stages of implementation, with a few hundred bots to date, it expects to have over a thousand bots deployed by year's end. Their bots automate sales order entry into its delivery systems.

Said Shukla:

> "Think of the impact of this on real estate requirements. I can take what would need offices in six large buildings and put them on two racks. I can help consolidate global offices. A cognitive bot can process an invoice in 30 languages—I don't need centers in the Philippines and other centers in Japan to deliver diverse language skills. Think of the employee recruiting and onboarding time we can help save."

About his Uber type ambition? "I think we will introduce two to three million cognitive bots into the workplace within the next five years."

Wine Science

Another hour south, in Salinas, Tyler Scheid explained the technology changes in an ancient industry tracing back to 6,000 BC:

> "Scheid Vineyards is involved in almost every single value stream that you can have in a winery. We sell bulk grapes as well as bulk wine to other wineries. We do custom crush, so we have wineries bring their fruit into our winery, where we process it and then send it back as juice. We'll do custom winemaking all the way from field to bottle. And we produce our own brands."

He catalogued their field machines:

> "Manual pruning is exhausting. Your arms and hands get tired, and our workforce is aging. With battery technology improving, we have moved to electronic pruners and special gloves to protect against injuries. It's safer, easier, and allows workers to focus on the cuts rather than just trying to get through the vine. The pruner now also generates data that provides additional analytics for our pruning operations management.
>
> Machine harvesters vibrate vines, which are anchored by the trellis system. Think of it as plucking a guitar string. When you have a properly maintained trellis system, it creates an environment where you're going to have an efficient machine pick. The machine captures the fruit as it falls, then it runs up a conveyor and over into a gondola.
>
> Knowing the details of what is in each gondola provides us a huge logistical benefit. In the past, it was a real challenge, especially when you're picking at night, to document the paperwork. Today, you wake up and you can immediately see how much fruit you picked from each field and how much is left. If you got a little bit higher yield than you thought you had, you could immediately start to make adjustments to your next schedule as well as plan to sell more fruit. Automating this data collection with yield monitoring is the next level of automation in harvest data capture that we're looking to solve. You have the immediate benefits for managing the logistics of a pick, as well as having a yield map output that provides a wealth of information for managing the next vintage crop.
>
> Then there is the traceability angle. Each truck has multiple gondolas. You can track that a truckload is 75% from this block and 25% from the block next to it. You can track a tank of wine all the way back out to the blocks they were sourced from. This is even after blending. You can track it

down to a pretty fine level of detail and basically see the field origin of a bottle of wine.

Harvesters are also getting more advanced, with sensors that can measure picking head status and RPMs. You can get a better picture of the health of the machine, so to speak. You can better maintain a piece of equipment before it breaks down."

Scheid got more excited when he described how machines are helping with irrigation in a state where water is increasingly a major concern:

"Now, at every single ranch we have a weather station that captures rainfall, temperature, humidity, solar radiation, wind speed, and direction. We have leveraged our onsite weather network for 20+ years, but just now are using this data to model plant stress and water status. We use a tool called Vintel, from a company called ITK, to do the modeling. It takes parameters such as root depth, canopy size, the major stages of plant growth, and helps us visualize our irrigation targets relative to modeled plant response. The modeling helps us gain more intelligence and value from our sensor assets.

Another automation we use focuses on controlling pumps at the well head, as well as turning valves in the field. We have installed what's called a variable frequency drive at a number of our wells. It also gives us control at the well head to activate the well remotely. We work with a company called Ranch Systems, as well as AgTech Industries, which provide farm-wide networks with wireless monitoring and control of the entire growing and irrigation cycle, plus add-ons like camera monitoring. The real benefit of automation is that we will have much more flexibility in the timing and the extent of changes and combinations, which may not be feasible within a workday for an irrigator to accomplish using manual systems. Automation will also allow our irrigators to focus more on crop and irrigation system health, rather than switching valves and monitoring set changes."

Scheid discussed other technologies that his company utilizes:

"We continue to work with imagery in the near-infrared part of the spectrum, as well as infrared, to calculate what they call a Normalized Difference Vegetation Index (NDVI). That is an index of plant 'greenness' or photosynthetic activity, and is one of the most commonly used vegetation indices. Such indices are based on observations that different surfaces reflect light differently. That's been around since the '70s. We need to advance this to another level to get more accurate and more robust vegetation indices for crops. In the next wave, I believe we'll see improvements in the postprocessing of imagery, so that the remote sensing data products are more easily interpreted and actionable for the nontechnical farmer, as well as more easily integrated within a modeling framework.

I look at the vineyard as a manufacturing plant. It just happens to use solar radiation as input, but it's essentially a factory, and the question is how best to optimize it. Some of the stuff that we do is not just winemaking, it's really resource management and managing the business side of the industry."

Scheid summarized by pointing out how winemaking is increasingly global:

"We go to Europe to look for technology, and then we host Europeans here in the US. The wine industry shares so much about technology that it's hard to say that anybody's ahead of another. Having said that, let me brag a bit about Scheid. We innovated a mobile press that rolls from the crush pad into the fermenter room and up to a conic bottom fermenter, so must (the juice) can be transferred with minimal disturbance and high labor efficiency. The conic bottom fermenter was also innovated by Scheid as part of the system. The custom designed access door is dubbed the 'Scheid Slide' and has been adopted by other wineries."

Every profession is being reshaped by automation and technology. The old terminology of white, blue, or brown collar is passé—we all live in the Silicon Collar economy.

"Wait a minute," you may say. "These are all examples from in and around the invigorating setting of Silicon Valley. Surely you cannot extrapolate that to the rest of the world." In the next chapter, we will examine jobs found in less hospitable settings.

CHAPTER 2

In Less Idyllic Settings

⌁→

While the examples in Chapter 1 come from the stimulating setting of Northern California, let's next look at automation technology deployed in more extreme and challenging environments.

In the risky oil patch

David Truch is tasked with automation in one such inhospitable environment. Truch is a technology director in BP's Digital Innovation Organization and his job, as he put it in an interview, is to evaluate "what some people call robotics but it's, broadly speaking, the capabilities that are being derived through the marriage of IT and a variety of STEM disciplines applied to craft in flight, ground, or water."

Truch described the scope and details of his oversight:

> "We work in environmentally harsh environments. The harshness comes in extremes of outside temperature, 105 degrees F above to 65 degrees F below, working in jungles and in places which are geopolitically challenging. Elsewhere, we work where you don't have decent infrastructure or, if you do, it doesn't last long. Of course, we also have to work in places where no human could ever get to—as with deep-water activity.
>
> There's another complication. We always have to worry about getting there and working there in a safe manner, which boils down to not using equipment that produces sparks. In our terminology, that's called "intrinsically safe."

Truch continued talking about the "state of the art" in the industry:

> "In some ways, our industry has been living for decades with papyrus and stylus, meaning we get a human out there with a clipboard and some paper and pencil capturing a bunch of data. Some of the locations in the world where we are, there is no communications infrastructure, no such thing as cell towers. At best, you can get access to a satellite for information transfer—but it's not cheap. In some cases, in the far north, there just isn't a lot in terms of a satellite constellation to get continuous coverage or continuous transmission of data.
>
> So our employees have to use ropes on rigs and climb to some very large elevations in order to be able to inspect things. As a consequence, the inspection process tends to be point focused in small areas of interest. It's what I call the observational world—a human looking at the information; a human making the interpretation of the delta from the last visit, and usually writing the results in text format; and maybe taking a few pictures of what they see.

Now, one can argue that all of our subsea activity had to be robotic-based because you can't put a human a mile deep in the water. Our surface stuff, yes, we still put humans and divers down a few hundred meters, but for the most part all of our subsea infrastructure and installation has always been done through high-cost, working class ROVs [remotely operated vehicles]."

Truch then discussed how, in the last few years, digital technology has improved their ability to communicate, and the ability to use robotic devices in the field.

"That is all changing now. We've done quite a bit of work with unmanned aerial vehicles. As a matter of fact, BP was the first company in North America the FAA has approved to fly a drone under a certificate of authority for pipeline monitoring. We also heavily utilized the Wave Glider technology for water quality monitoring in the Gulf of Mexico.

Instead of having to have someone use challenging approaches to collecting data in hard to reach areas, I can send a robotic crawler. I can collect the same information, and I can collect it in digital form. That's where real value is starting to come in—the human eye can only comprehend certain things, it can only see them at a certain amount of resolution, and it can only detect something when it gets to a certain point of degradation. It is very hard for a human eye to see pinholes, small blisters, or flaking of a coating. These days, when that data can be converted into a digital format we can use pattern recognition, vision recognition algorithms, and set highly accurate baselines.

The second aspect is that instead of spot measurements we can now gather far more, an almost continuous coverage. So I can take images of the entire length of pipe. And because it is digital, the next time I go there, I can start calculating deltas. I can detect change through the lens of the digital algorithms instead of the lens of the human eye.

The major goal of automation for inspections and monitoring is that we can improve people safety. It doesn't remove the human's involvement, but they don't have to dangle from ropes, fly low over remote pipelines trying to record observations, or drive hundreds of miles away from humanity to perform inspections. Eventually, a lot of these things we'll be able to do with the human quite far physically out of the loop, meaning they could be back in some major city monitoring and operating these things from afar."

He described some of the technologies they have been testing and how they are gradually improving:

"We are working with sensor manufacturers up and down the electromagnetic spectrum to gather information about the integrity of our infrastructures. Subsea is still a challenge—once one acquires data, how do we communicate that back to where we can start analyzing it?

The FAA took several years to approve drone usage. In that time span there have been significant technological improvements. In my view, we're probably on the seventh generation of drone air frames. We have seen significant improvement in optical cameras and the miniaturization of sensor packages. The FAA is now starting to relax its rules. We still have challenges because we still cannot go beyond line of sight, but we have plenty of elevated infrastructure where people used to climb towers and stacks. Drones can inspect that within line of sight, and we are starting to reap the benefits.

We need timelines of three or four hours of flight from certain vehicles, where today the range is only 20 minutes. You supplement that with remote sensing technology from satellites, and high-flying balloons, and altitude aircraft at

60,000-plus feet that can stay up for quite a long period of time. I see this tiered approach where we can have extremely broad coverage, get to areas of interest where I may decide to deploy more drones that are flying in the 400-feet range, rather than the 60,000 foot or satellite range, and focus on a much narrower area of 10 square kilometers but with much greater accuracy.

As we have swarms of drones collecting data, it is going to take far more compute power to process all the data. It's going to take cloud-based approaches, maybe even quantum computing, but it very definitely will also take a lot of improvements in the learning algorithms to understand change detection at that level of detail.

When it comes to robotics, it's good to see DARPA Challenges (the prize competitions sponsored by the US Defense agency) moving to the actuation side: "Okay. If you're there and you do see something wrong can you fix it right then and there?" So we welcome that, but today there is very little in the way of robotic actuation—other than subsea, because they had to be designed for nonhuman actuation. It was designed for, essentially, our working-class ROV approaches.

And, of course, we have to be very focused on intrinsic safety. The closer we get to the heart of operations, the more we have to ensure that there's an intrinsically safe type of technology, whether it's flying or crawling or walking, it cannot be generating sparks."

How is all this automation affecting workers?

"We are telling inspectors they can spend far more of their time on looking at the analysis of the data they are collecting, and far less on worrying about whether they're getting a good collection. Yes, I'm changing the nature of your job, and I think I'm making it more interesting."

The Fourth Industrial Revolution

To many, the shop floor is far from idyllic.

Every January, a group of global movers and shakers—politicians, business executives, academics, and celebrities—descend on the exclusive Swiss ski resort of Davos Klosters, to be part of the annual meeting of the World Economic Forum. German economist Klaus Schwab founded the WEF in 1971 with an ambitious goal: to make the world a better place.

The agenda for 2016 was "Mastering the Fourth Industrial Revolution." The first three revolutions came with its introduction of mechanization, electricity, and IT. Now, Big Data, the Internet of Things, robotics, and other technologies are allowing for another revolution—and hopefully making the world an even better place.

The WEF is usually ahead of the curve when it comes to such thinking. In this case, however, its cue came from a concept called "Industrie 4.0" that Germany has been pioneering for a few years. In 2013, Karl-Heinz Streibich, CEO of Software AG, Germany's second-largest software company (after SAP), invited me to collaborate on his book *The Digital Enterprise*.[13] In the book, you can read about a wide range of business executives and academics who mention Industrie 4.0 and discuss how factories, transportation, stores, and how the jobs around each are being transformed.

Dr. Henning Kagermann, former CEO of SAP and now President of acatech, the German National Academy of Science and Engineering, told me how German industry has been balancing labor concerns about these technologies. In the book he was quoted:

> "Trade unions have historically been uneasy about automation and technology. Charlie Chaplin expressed these fears brilliantly in his 1936 classic, *Modern Times*. To mollify these

---

[13] https://www.amazon.com/Digital-Enterprise-Karl-Heinz-Streibich/dp/0989756408/ref=sr_1_1?ie=UTF8&qid=1467474798&sr=8-1&keywords=the+digital+enterprise

fears, we had to explain to union members that the next-generation agile robot is more of a personal assistant that actually gives workers more flexibility in performing their jobs. Unlike the previous generation of large, noisy robots in cages, these agile robots actually help create more pleasant working environments. Further, given Germany's aging workforce, these 'assistants' allow the country to remain globally competitive. Going further, greener factories, which can be located closer to the towns and cities where workers live, encourage a better work/life balance."

When he mentions global competition, Kagermann particularly means China, which is looking way past Industrie 4.0 as it plans for future manufacturing with its "Made in China 2025" initiative. It is being put in practice by Foxconn, which is best known as the Apple contract manufacturer for products like its iPhone. Foxconn is a diverse company which also plays in automobile, health care, and other markets. Its 1.3 million employees, many in China, work alongside its custom-built Foxbots, at the cutting edge of automation in various manufacturing contexts. A customer executive describing Foxconn said, "Not only are they good at making stuff, they are also good at stuff that makes the stuff."

You can also see it in the U.S., which is enjoying its own manufacturing renaissance. Jason Blessing, CEO of the cloud-manufacturing software vendor Plex, described to an audience of his customers what he had heard from a friend who had been at Davos:

"He starts talking about the factory of the future. In the future, we're going to have clean modern factories, and the shop floors are going to network machines and mobile devices that are tied together with ubiquitous access. In the future, we're going to have these things called smart sensors, which will read critical production data to allow assembly lines to automatically report issues to operators so they can take corrective action. In the future, we're going to have this technology called wearable technology. These are going to be purpose-built devices that workers wear. It will make jobs easier and safer. Make labor more efficient. In the future, we're going to have these things called smart products. These are products that will phone home and report issues in the field that will enable engineers to either change product design or perhaps change the manufacturing process. In the future, we're going to have sophisticated reporting, to make sense of all this data that's being collected. It's going to allow all of you to make more informed decisions on everything from supply chain planning to preventative maintenance.

I let him continue. I was hoping to hear something mind-bending. As he finished, he looked at me ready for this grand reaction. I grabbed his arm, and I said 'You know what? I've seen this future. I see this future every day. I see this future every day when I go to work. This future is now.'

Many of you in this room, the Plex community, you're doing these things. It dawned on me the magnitude of what we're doing together. What we're doing, the Plex community, is someday going to be taught in classrooms. In a sense, we're the pioneers who are leading the fourth industrial revolution—leveraging technology to make manufacturing plants more intelligent, safe, and efficient than ever."

Plex's customers are pragmatic about automation. They have been doing it for decades. Paul Wright, CIO at Accuride, told me:

"We have vibration sensors deployed across our environment. We're just starting to plug some of that information into Plex. It's about putting those quality systems online. So it's not just about the defect—that's downtime related now. It's about a defect that's quality related, it's getting immediately to the quality team. It's about then, them being able to broadcast messages to our Plex stations on the shop floor, to say, 'Here's a quality alert, this is happening in this part of the plant, please look out for this everywhere.' Everything is loaded with scanners, but they're all the handheld scanners right now. We haven't gone into the finger scanners because in our environment, with these big, heavy things, it's not like someone is pushing things around on a cart, where a linked scanner would make a lot more sense for them. For us, the driver is always on his forklift, and so we put the visual display on the forklift, so basically there's a full mobile PC environment that links up to the Bluetooth scanner that he's got on his truck. But we are only going to add layers of technology at Accuride when we think it adds something back to the process, that we can use it to effectively communicate both into and out of Plex. So as soon as we're done implementing new plants, I think we get to do another round, and do a bunch of fun stuff."

Tim Cripsey, another Plex customer, is a plant General Manager with MFC Netform, which forms metal components used for power trains in automotive and agriculture. The spotless plant emphasizes 5S manufacturing (a lean manufacturing methodology), and blends "operator-led" autonomy with several Fanuc robots which do many of the dirty and dangerous tasks. The plant proudly displays a giant "Made in Detroit" sign above the floor. Cripsey told me:

"With robots, you are changing the nature of the job. They take away lower level, often unsafe activities, but generate higher paying, more skilled trade level and programming jobs. You need an infrastructure to maintain and reprogram the machines. We have not automated on a purely fiscal basis. It's always been tied to situations which are dangerous to workers such as in machine loading or in deburring situations."

Like Dr. Kagermann, Cripsey sees robots evolving to serve collaborative roles such as co-bots like Baxter, a two-armed industrial robot with a base price of $25,000:

> "Not only are they more attractive from a cost perspective; they are also easier to train and deploy than today's robots. As you see on our floor, the Fanuc robots are extremely well guarded with interlocks. This next generation, with their sensors, should be able to work beside you without the danger of getting humans hurt. If you gave them a bit of a character, as stupid as this sounds, give them names and faces, you'd almost make them personable and acceptable. To me, that's a very interesting future."

Beyond Robotics

Another manufacturing example comes from artisans in Italy who have come under pressure due to competition from places like China and India. *Business Week* described how 3-D printing is allowing for a resurgence:

> "Pomini teamed up with Selvaggia Armani, an artist and designer. The two began working on a series of lamps designed by Armani and manufactured to order on Pomini's 3D printers. The pieces—some of which include intricate meshwork or interlocking chains that would be difficult to produce using traditional methods—take shape slowly, each layer fused from powdered nylon by a high-power laser. The project was a surprising success: Pomini now works with more than a dozen designers; he introduced 3D printed jewelry in 2012. 'This is the beauty of this technology,' says Armani, 47. 'You can build things that are impossible.' Techniques such as the 3D printing used by Pomini and Armani have helped turn northeastern Italy into an unlikely

hothouse of innovation. Last year growth in the region was positive for the first time since 2007."[14]

It's not just on the manufacturing shop floor. Jeff Immelt, CEO of GE, the U.S. diversified company, has called his locomotives "rolling data centers." For the Streibich book, we had also interviewed Bill Ruh of GE, and he described the vast potential that the company's "Industrial Internet" (their version of Industrie 4.0 described above) holds for many other industries. He is quoted in the Streibich book:

> "1% of aviation fuel savings is US $30 billion over 15 years. 1% in better optimization of healthcare facilities adds US $63 billion over 15 years. 1% reduction in oil and gas CAPEX adds another US $90 billion."

Jeremiah Stone, general manager for Asset Performance Management (APM) at GE Digital, said:

> "Companies that wait for equipment to fail spend an average of 13% of replacement asset value annually on maintenance. Companies that employ proactive condition-based maintenance, by contrast, face a slim cost of just 2%."[15]

Workers at airport hangars, wind turbine farms, hospitals, and many other settings are seeing the growing impact of smarter GE machines that generate loads of data which is then acted upon. Indeed, the fastest-growing job category, according to the BLS, is wind turbine service technicians.

---

[14] http://www.bloomberg.com/news/features/2015-05-05/how-3-d-printing-is-saving-the-italian-artisan

[15] http://www.gereports.com/how-the-third-wave-of-the-internet-is-stoking-the-second-machine-age/

On the Battlefield

Want yet more hostile work environments?

It is a morbid business, but throughout most of history, soldiers have benefited from new technology, and that technology often ends up in commercial applications.

In her book about DARPA, *The Pentagon's Brain*, Annie Rasmussen documents a wide range of technologies that have helped the last couple of generations of U.S. soldiers. She discusses sensors—seismic, infrared, acoustic, and other types—and their deployment in the Vietnam War. Later generations of such sensors are helping workers in today's Internet of Things and the previously discussed Fourth Industrial Revolution. She discusses TALON robots and their role in detonating land mines and IEDs (improvised explosive devices). Soldiers affectionately give them human names. Their robotic cousins are helping today in many industrial applications, especially on the shop floor. She discusses the role of drones in the first U.S./Iraq war in 1991, and today many industries (like the oil industry Truch described previously) are finding logistics, inspection, crop-dusting, and other applications for them.

Conversely, in some cases the military has benefited from technologies that came from the consumer world. The Norwegian military, for example, is testing a new system that utilizes the Oculus Rift—the Facebook virtual reality headset—to get a full view of the battlefield from inside a tank. This use case could be adapted to other tight spaces where human movement is constrained.

In other cases, the inspiration comes from Hollywood. The *Iron Man* movie series has regenerated interest in exoskeletons. The U.S. military has a research project around the Tactical Assault Light Operator Suit, or TALOS. Soon after the movie *Avatar* was released, DARPA announced its own Avatar program, which "will develop interfaces and algorithms to enable a soldier to effectively partner with a semiautonomous bipedal machine and allow it to act as the soldier's surrogate."[16] As has been the pattern with other technologies, workers somewhere, somehow will find it useful on their jobs within a few decades.

The slogan "Army of One" has been adapted by many private sector recruiters—it shows the growing help individual contributors, not just soldiers, are getting from all the technologies that surround them.

The Battle for Technology Budgets

Then there is the white collar war that is being waged in many an enterprise.

The analyst firm Gartner has predicted that by 2017, the Chief Marketing Officer will have a bigger technology budget than the Chief Information Officer.[17] You can argue about the timeline, but there is no question that the marketing role has become increasingly digital with the growth of social media, email campaigns, and interactive billboards.

Steve Mann, former CMO of LexisNexis North America and now head of AbleBrains LLC, a digital marketing consultancy, says we have moved to the mash-up of neuroscience and digital marketing, so-called "neuro-digital marketing," the ability to speak to the nonconscious in influencing consumers. Mann described the process:

> "Our pleasure centers are driven by dopamine, as are our motor functions. And while endorphins [morphine-like neurochemicals that stimulate our pleasure centers] make us like something, dopamine makes us want more of it.
>
> Would you choose a wine based on the music you're hearing? The logical answer is, 'Of course not!' But behavioral economist Antonio Rangel conducted an experiment at a

---

supermarket which showed that on days French music was playing, 77% of the wine purchased was French. On days German music was played, 73% of the wine purchased was German. Buyers were influenced by a *factor*—the music—which delivered a nonconscious impression and drove purchase choice.

In another Rangel wine study, identical wines were marked with a price of either $90 or $10. When subjects knew the prices, they perceived the $90 wine as superior. But during blind taste tests, the subjects rated the wines as identical! More significantly, when the brains of these subjects were fMRI scanned while drinking the $90 wine, their brains showed more activity in the area associated with the experience of pleasure—the orbito-frontal cortex—than when drinking the $10 bottle."

As shown in Rangel's fMRI wine study, product preferences can be driven by pleasure center stimulation. And dopamine drives desire for that product.

Mann continued:

"Gamification is a great example of how neurodigital marketing speaks to the nonconscious to drive preference for a product and its experience. My wife is completely addicted to Sudoku. She receives an immense amount of satisfaction from playing, and it isn't just because of the feeling of joy she receives when she solves a puzzle. The actual key to her addiction, or any gamer's addiction, is to create expectations of something not just rewarding but surprising. She is constantly surprised by the unknown variations in the games she's served after winning a game . . . Killer Sudoku, Clock Sudoku, Irregular Sudoku, 4×4s, 6×6s, 12×12s. Bottom line? She doesn't know what the next game will bring in terms of challenge or type. These unknown future games stimulate her desire for more of whatever is giving her pleasure."

Mann then provided an example from the complex world of enterprise software:

"SAP launched the SAP Community Network (SCN) over a decade ago. It has grown to become the premier online community for customers, employees, consultants, professional services firms, and outsourcers in the SAP ecosystem. Information about SAP products and services is shared in the community, as are deep discussions around the intricacies of deploying SAP software. However, when SCN transitioned to a new community platform a few years back, the SAP team immediately faced a problem they didn't expect: member engagement indicators dropped dramatically.

Rather than risk losing members or having to reengage and remarket to them, the team chose to gamify the SCN experience by designing 'missions' community members could pursue. These missions were surprise, reward-oriented achievements, just like a viral game, and are meant to stimulate our pleasure centers. In pursuing missions, community members earned points that increased their reputation within the community. For example, missions included onboarding to the community, contributing content, showcasing expertise, or influencing peers.

Members were enticed to desire *more*—more influence, peer admiration, and respect—because of the surprise nature of the missions they were served. The SAP team initially launched about 30 missions. In true gaming strategy fashion, future missions were hidden until the prior mission was completed. This created the surprise element that is so important to engaging the dopamine/endorphin reward complex.

The preliminary results observed just one month after the launch were impressive:

- Activity within the community increased by 400%.

- A 2,210% jump in activity-generating points, which indicates how much gamification drove contributions and engagement around content.

- Community feedback rose by 96%.

- A total of 53,028 badges were earned after completion of missions.

Gamifying SCN filled the community with engagement addicts driven by each member's *pleasure center.*"

Mann chuckled, "If being addicted to SCN makes you happy, then more power to you."

Robo-Writers

Another type of hostile setting is one which journalists sometimes face.

Think of the digital cloak and dagger behind what is being called "The Panama Papers." The Washington, DC-based International Consortium of Investigative Journalists collected a massive data trove, then coordinated with more than a hundred media outlets around the world. The confidential records—2.6 terabytes of data, or more than 11.5 million documents—leaked from the Panamanian law firm Mossack Fonseca by an anonymous source has exposed scores of global leaders and their offshore bank accounts.

Over months, encrypted communications and crypto-apps like Signal and Threema helped in masking such a large initiative. This database is far larger than the intelligence records revealed by Edward Snowden in 2013 or the U.S. diplomatic cables made public by WikiLeaks in 2010. While jaws were dropping about the wealth these leaders appear to be hiding, even more striking is the fact that a group of journalists had managed such an impressive digital effort.

Many journalists also face a hostile economic environment, with everyone predicting the end of print media. Dennis Howlett is proof that it has not died, but rather has evolved with digital tools.

Howlett spent his early career in various finance-related roles. He then got into journalism, helping launch *Information Week* in the UK and contributing to a variety of business and technology magazines and journals. Next, he was a prolific blogger for ZDNet.

Three years ago, he launched Diginomica along with several other bloggers including Phil Wainewright, who had previously launched a site called ASPNews.com in the late '90s. Diginomica has rapidly become a "go to" source for readers who want to hear about enterprise technologies from SAP, Oracle, and others. But running their own publishing business has meant its team has become a set of digital experts.

Howlett told me:

> "The days of cranking out copy into a Word document and throwing it over the digital wall to an editor are long gone. Today's digital journalist has to be skilled at crafting, editing, fact-checking, sourcing appropriate images and/or video, checking for copyright issues, checking for formatting problems, and then publishing into a CMS [content management system]. All in real time. Thankfully, the days of needing to know much HTML are over since most modern CMS hide the complexities behind a visual editor but if you're a lone publisher with aspirations of scale, then things are very different. You quickly discover that HTML alone won't get you very far.
>
> While there are thousands of stock templates from which to choose, most of them come with baggage that will kill your site stone dead once you reach scale. We found that out the hard way once our site passed 100,000 readers per month.

The same goes for plug-ins, many of which are 'supported' under free-to-use licenses. Good luck with that when the developer decides they've had enough of 'free' and need to earn a living. Or worse still, a plug-in upgrade crashes your site or contains malware. We know, for example, that a Facebook tracker can place a DoubleClick pixel onto your site. You won't know that unless you use a tool like Ghostery to discover what's running on your site. Of course, DoubleClick might be just the thing you need if your site is advertising supported, but with ad blockers now passing 200 million in use, ad support is no longer sustainable for many publishers.

Today, we believe the modern publisher requires at least a passing knowledge of PHP, Javascript, and CSS so they can integrate functionality directly into the core of their platform. Hosting at a place that directly supports your chosen CMS is a must. We've been through three of them in as many years, changing as our needs evolved. We've moved away from in-house coding, to first having a tech support person, and now a full service agency managing design, implementation, and support. If that sounds over the top then, sure, it will be for most lone publishers, but not if you are building something that has many users and readers."

Jon Reed, another member of the Diginomica team, got to know Howlett via a video site they created. Howlett described the video technology expertise they had acquired:

"When we jumped into the video creation pool, equipment had already plummeted in price to a point where for less than $35,000 you could set up a portable broadcast studio capable of producing high-quality content. At the minimum, you need prosumer quality cameras like the Canon XA-10s we use, a broadcast switcher from vendors like Livestream or NewTek, good lighting, preferably controllable LED, and professional grade audio gear. We use high-quality Sennheiser wireless mics for on-the-couch interviews linked back to our NewTek Tricaster via a digital mixing board.

We recently replicated the studio for a remote location and were able to set it up for less than $25,000, including lighting and switcher upgrades and an IP broadcast unit that allows us to deliver high-quality, real-time, Skype-based conversations.

All of this can be run by a single person using a dedicated iPad application but it is always better to have a studio engineer on hand to ensure that everything is running correctly."

Diginomica also has guest contributors like Charlie Bess, whose entire career has focused on automation activities. He had a ham radio license by the sixth grade. Growing up on a farm was a solitary life, and the radio allowed him to connect with the rest of the world. It also created a lifelong passion for technical discovery while learning how farms were being automated. Bess was a HP Fellow, working on several artificial intelligence projects. He is on the executive board of the US-FIRST Robotics Competition in North Texas, coordinating competition judging.

Bess took a somewhat clinical view on how technology is reshaping journalism:

"Today, writing a sports story about a baseball game is 100% automatable. You can make it so that almost nobody could tell the difference if it is an automated version, or that a sports journalist wrote it. Some people might be offended by that. I'm not saying that sportswriters should go away. They have their place, but is it not better to have thousands of baseball games covered versus hundreds that the traditional sportswriter could cover effectively? That's one of the things with automation—you can scale massively."

He is talking about tools like Quill, which collates data on thousands of these games and can produce thousands of articles almost instantaneously, one for each game. Professor Larry Birnbaum, inventor of the Quill writing tool, said, "Computers have known how to write in English for years. The reason they haven't done so in the past is they had nothing to say, lacking access to a sufficient volume of information."[18] Now they have interesting stories to tell humans, and the Associated Press has been using robo-journalism for sports stories and earnings reports for years, using tools like Wordsmith. *Wired* magazine wrote nearly five years ago about a similar technology: "Niche news services hire Narrative Science to write updates for their subscribers, be they sports fans, small-cap investors, or fast-food franchise owners."[19]

Since 2013, a team of computer scientists led by Hitoshi Matsubara of Future University Hakodate in Hokkaido has been trying to get artificial intelligence-based computers to write fiction. They recently entered a computer-generated short story titled "A day when a computer writes fiction" for the Hoshi Literary prize in Japan.[20]

Virtual Contracting

Yet another potentially hostile setting is in the legal practice. LexisNexis, through its Lex Machina acquisition, promises to reveal "insights"—some may call them biases—"never before available about judges, lawyers, parties, and patents, culled from millions of pages of IP litigation information."[21]

---

[18] http://www.theguardian.com/technology/2014/sep/12/artificial-intelligence-data-journalism-media
[19] http://www.wired.com/2012/04/can-an-algorithm-write-a-better-news-story-than-a-human-reporter/
[20] http://www.japantimes.co.jp/news/2016/06/19/national/science-health/japanese-researchers-take-artificial-intelligence-toward-the-final-frontier-creativity/#.V2qJwvkrJD9
[21] https://lexmachina.com/

Bill Hewitt, an American, is CEO of Exari, which was founded 15 years ago by two corporate lawyers and a technologist in Australia.

Their basic thesis was that the traditional contracting process has been slow, cumbersome, and error-prone. Companies were disenchanted with the fact that they would create the same documents over and over again, and they would require a lawyer to create each one. Exari has created a "machine" to extract key data from contracts and deliver insights instantaneously. They have created a Universal Contract Model™ that can harmonize any contract, regardless of the form, language, or style.

Hewitt explained why that is important:

> "Contracts are intended to be business tools, and today most contracts are artifacts and only exposed when something goes wrong. The fact is, if companies could operationalize their contract data, they would not miss revenue opportunities and would be 100% informed as to the risk of their contract portfolio.
>
> Take a nondisclosure agreement (NDA), which is the single most used contract form, and based on how you answered the questions you might choose a duration of one, two, or three years. You might choose one-way or mutual. You might choose what kind of tail you have in the confidentiality and what to do with any confidential information at the end of the period. All those things can generate 40, 50 and 60 different variations. With Exari, it's all done with one wizard-driven 'interview.'
>
> As our company got more involved with bigger customers, we started working on very complex agreements like the International Swaps and Derivatives Association (ISDA) Master Agreement. After the financial crisis, this form was deemed to be the standard form, and it's still heavily negotiated. In many cases it can be 50, 60, or 70 pages, so we

now drive that ISDA creation, and things like investment management agreements, credit support annexes, and other types of trading documents for some of the biggest banks in the world.

Users started to ask us, 'Can we look at the data in these contracts across our entire contract asset base?' Going back to our NDA as an example—how many of these are in the jurisdiction of Delaware, or New York, or Massachusetts? How many of our sales agreements have termination for convenience, or have limitations of liability that are outside of what we want to write in our contracts? We realized that they could use the exact same technology to decompose a contract that they used to construct it. Using the same interview construct, a user would go through and execute a contract, answer the questions, and not only capture the physical document itself, but now capture the normalized data that's in that contract. When I say normalized data, that's the important part, because, as everybody knows, contracts are highly interpretive, and one contract could have 10 paragraphs in a limitations-of-liability clause while another might have two, yet they could say the exact same thing.

Our vision is a world where the contract process is virtual. Companies negotiate with each other in cyberspace, taking best practices from a universal library of clauses and precedents or recommendations from a contract 'machine.' Automatic scoring of risk gives the negotiator visibility into how exposed they are, allowing them to ensure they are putting proper protections in place. Finally, the contract is analyzed against similar previous contracts and the libraries are updated even as the contract whizzes through cyberspace with electronic counterparty signatures. The contract and its core data are stored, and now are ready to inform downstream and upstream systems of the new rights and obligations.

That future is not that far off."

Computational Chemistry

Yet another potentially unsafe area is the chemistry lab.

With its sprawling campus, Texas A&M in College Station has boasted Cray, Silicon Graphics, IBM, and other supercomputers for over a quarter century, each new one breaking previous records of impressive computational prowess. In its physics, meteorology, nuclear engineering, and other advanced STEM areas, Texas A&M researchers have benefited from this high-performance computing power. One beneficiary today is the Wheeler Group, headed by Prof. Steven Wheeler. The Group's website explains, "most of our efforts are directed towards distilling computational data into conceptual, predictive models to explain various chemical phenomena. What we are after is insight, not numbers."

Dr. Wheeler's particular focus is computational quantum chemistry. In an interview, he told me:

> "Computational chemistry is complementary to experimental work in the lab. There are aspects of chemical behavior that we can predict computationally but are difficult or impossible to observe experimentally. As an example, there are molecules that wouldn't be stable other than in outer space.
>
> Down on an atomic level, the motion of electrons is governed by quantum mechanics, so we're solving the equations of quantum mechanics that predict what the electrons are doing in molecules, which determines their molecular property, their reactivity, and how they interact with each other.
>
> In that interaction, there's what we call a transition state. It's the least stable structure as they go from reactants to products. Experimentally, it exists but for less than a femtosecond [a quadrillionth of a second], but we can use quantum mechanics to calculate the structure of that transition state, and to predict its properties. We are constantly looking

at transition states, the reactions, in order to explain why reactions go a certain way, to and from a certain product."

He provided some historical perspective:

"Quantum chemistry was born more or less when quantum mechanics was born. Schrödinger, Heisenberg, and Dirac helped define quantum mechanics in the mid '20s (and all three qualified for Nobel Prizes in physics a few years later). By 1928, there was a paper (by Linus Pauling at CalTech) that was applying quantum mechanics to hydrogen, the simplest of molecules. That was the birth of molecular quantum mechanics. Obviously, for the next few decades there were no computers, so people did calculations either by hand, or on a mechanical calculator, and then as electronic calculators and computers came onto the scene we have been able to tackle far more complex molecules. The molecules we were looking at when I was a grad student, starting in 2001 or 2002, are tiny compared to what we can look at now, just because of the growth of computing power.

There was a bit of overoptimism in the 1980s that computational chemistry was going to make drug design a trivial process. As the '90s progressed into the 2000s, we realized that the problem was much harder than it appeared. Computational chemistry can predict certain properties of how drugs will function, but they can't solve the whole problem."

As computational power has grown, so have applications—as we saw with the bioinformatics at Hampton Creek in Chapter 1:

"Computational chemists are working on how to take an existing enzyme, a protein that catalyzes a reaction, and modify it so it catalyzes a reaction that's potentially more useful industrially. We are trying to develop computational tools that will let us screen potential catalyst designs. The way things work today, synthetic organic chemists, people who actually make molecules, dream up a few dozen different potential catalysts on paper or on a marker board. Then they go and make each one, and test whether or not it works. It's a tedious, time-consuming process. We are developing tools that will let us test the molecules computationally. We may not get to 100% accuracy, but even if we have 80% accuracy, it's significant. If a synthetic chemist comes down to a list of a hundred catalysts, we can say, 'These 80 are never going to work. It's a waste of time to make them. Focus on the other 20.' We could save them a week or a month's worth of work trying to do something that's just not thermodynamically possible.

Even someone who spends 99% of their time in the lab, making molecules—I think they're still more valuable because they are able to talk and communicate with computational chemists. Even if they can't run their own calculations, they at least know the basics, and they know, 'Oh, I can go ask a computational chemist.' They know what questions to ask, and things like that. At A&M, we teach a molecular modeling course that's taken almost entirely by experimental chemists.

Occasionally, I run into some people that don't trust computational chemistry. It likely goes back to the 1980s when computational chemistry was overhyped and I think a few people got disenfranchised or disappointed in it. But from a talent point of view, if I was evaluating two equally talented synthetic chemists, but one also knew calculations, then I would certainly hire the person that could also run the computations."

Urban Renewal?

Our roads are incredibly unsafe, with over 30,000 deaths from vehicle accidents in the U.S. every year.

Dr. Russell Fricano teaches urban planning at Minnesota State University (Mankato). Before his teaching career, he had spent two decades as a regional planner in car-dependent Los Angeles County, and has a good perspective on how technology has changed the planner's job:

"When I began my planning career and we analyzed a site, we used Mylar sheets that had different layers of information. Some sheets showed topography, others displayed environmental areas, roads, and infrastructure. You put them all together on a light table, and you tried to figure out the various attributes of the property as a composite. Doing so would give you major headaches. Today, we have Geographic Information Systems (GIS). GIS is a way of compiling in a digital format various features that you can map. It basically organizes a collection of digitized map-related information and it's capable of holding and using data describing places on the Earth's surface.

At the press of a button now, when you look at a site, you can find information on various physical characteristics of the site, whether they're environmental areas, seismic zones, zoning districts, and the comprehensive plan policies related to the site. It's all in one place, and it also compiles information in a spreadsheet format. GIS is also a part of an even larger system called Planning Support Systems (PSS). PSS is a package that integrates land use modeling, transportation modeling, and GIS. By using various mathematical models you can forecast, and also allocate future land use. You can use GIS to map proposed land use changes.

Planning has also been able to take advantage of remote sensing with satellite sensor technology. Whether it be from an aerial photo or a satellite, planners can obtain crisp 3-D resolution of terrain which is orthorectified for camera lens distortion. You can assess land use much more accurately.

Also, thanks to GPS, you can provide a digital map with a very high degree of accuracy, down to less than an inch.

While I am on the topic of computer technology, planning also benefits from storage technology and optical devices which scan and store historical map and case processing information. Digital archiving not only preserves information, but it also frees up a considerable amount of storage space once devoted to paper case files.

Planning also relies on interactive expert systems which provide regulatory and land use information to development applicants online, reducing the need for trips to the planning office, and making information available to remote locations."

Dr. Fricano then talked about how the state of the art continues to evolve:

"Technology is an integral part of the planning job today. If you take the certification exam of the American Planning Association, you are expected to be familiar with the latest technology.

And planning has gone global. You see digital smart signs on highways with accident and other traffic information. That was something we borrowed from Europe, but it's now very much part of our everyday life. It assists you when you drive, and smoothes out the traffic flow.

Perhaps the most effective strategy available to mitigate traffic congestion is charging motorists who travel in peak-hour traffic. We refer to this as 'congestion tolling.' Technology makes this possible. Singapore implemented Electronic Road Pricing (ERP) in 1998. Through the use of a prepaid debit card and a special device in vehicles, the city is able to monitor and charge commuters tolls that correspond to the level of congestion they travel in."

As if all that change was not dramatic enough, urban planners increasingly have to keep up with citizens who use real-time traffic pattern information from navigation apps like Waze.

School Education

To many, our schools have become war zones.

Teachers in K-12 schools have nowhere near the supercomputing resources Dr. Wheeler has access to at Texas A&M. In fact, they are perennially underfunded. Tony Prophet, Corporate Vice President of Education Marketing at Microsoft, is tasked with bringing new digital education experiences to the 1.5 billion teachers and students in primary and secondary education around the world.

The goal is to evolve beyond the three "R"s of traditional school education—reading, writing, and 'rithmetic—to the modern five "C"s. The National Education Association[22] has identified the first four Cs as part of its framework for 21st century learning: creativity, collaboration, critical thinking, and communication. With Microsoft, they are also helping emphasize a fifth C, which represents computational thinking.

Prophet has spent a lifetime watching and influencing automation trends. He started his career at GM in car assembly, and wrote an undergraduate thesis on robotics. He then spent several years at Booz Allen helping clients with complex supply chain strategies. Next, he helped architect the global supply chain operation at HP.

I described Prophet's impact at HP in a case study in *The New Technology Elite:*

> "It is a massive operation, the largest in the technology industry, with over $60 billion in components, warehouse, transportation, and other logistics costs. The HP machine churns out two personal computers a second, two printers a second, and a data center server every 15 seconds. It is

---

[22] http://www.nea.org/tools/52217.htm

also a constantly evolving operation with a changing mix of company-owned factories and contract manufacturing utilizing air/ship/rail logistics from/to most countries around the world."

When you sit down with Prophet, he can tell stories about the seasonal migration of talent in China, and how that has evolved with HP's pioneering expansion into Western China, which contains "70% of its land mass, 30% of its population, but just 20% of its total economic output." He talks about how HP's investment in the western city of Chongqing led to massive infrastructure investments—a nonstop, all-freight rail line to the port city of Shenzhen, extensions to the airport runways to allow fully laden 747s (with merchandise and extra fuel) to fly nonstop to Europe, and the opening of the "Silk Road"—a rail service that connects Western China to Europe.

In his role at Microsoft, Prophet explains how the company's tools and devices are helping teachers. The Torkinmäki School in Finland uses OneNote Class Notebook as a central collaboration space, a content library to store class materials (handwriting, text, web content, even audio and video) and an individual notebook for every student in the class that teachers can see in real time to provide feedback. Skype in the Classroom is allowing classrooms in California to connect with schools in New Zealand and elsewhere, and take students on virtual field trips. Sway is a storytelling app that makes it quick and easy to create polished, interactive lessons, assignments, reports, newsletters, and more—from any device.

The BBC micro:bit, supported by Microsoft, is aimed at virtually every Year 7 student (ages 11–12) in the UK. It is a wearable computing device, smaller than a credit card, that students can use to explore the possibilities of computing.

The *New York Times* described the emerging generation which is learning to code using Microsoft's Minecraft with an anecdote about a young student named Jordan:

"Jordan had used the cow's weird behavior to create, in effect, a random-number generator inside Minecraft. It was an ingenious bit of problem-solving, something most computer engineers I know would regard as a great hack—a way of coaxing a computer system to do something new and clever."[23]

Microsoft is also contributing to higher education with the goal of making degree programs much more affordable and speedier. It will offer its Microsoft Professional Degree (MPD) program through Edx.org, the Harvard/MIT-founded, not-for-profit online learning platform with most courses costing under $100. Those "going full throttle to gain their MPD could fire through a course per week, assuming that they're putting in around five hours each day, meaning they could gain their Data Science degree within 10 weeks."[24]

Other technology companies like Facebook are similarly helping teachers around the world. In a blog post, Facebook CEO Mark Zuckerberg explained its ambitious plans to bring connectivity:

"Today, only 2.7 billion people—a little more than one third of the world's population—have internet access. Even more surprising, internet adoption is growing by less than 9% each year, which is slow considering how early we are in its development and that it is expected to slow further. There are more than 5 billion mobile phones in the world, with almost 4 billion feature phones and more than 1 billion smartphones. As smartphone prices come down, many people who currently have feature phones will be able to afford smartphones over the next 5 years.

---

[23] http://www.nytimes.com/2016/04/17/magazine/the-minecraft-generation .html?_r=0
[24] http://venturebeat.com/2016/07/14/microsoft-launches-data-science-degree-to-plug-the-skills-gap-more-courses-could-follow/

We believe it's possible to sustainably provide free access to basic internet services in a way that enables everyone with a phone to get on the internet and join the knowledge economy while also enabling the industry to continue growing profits and building out this infrastructure. Today, the global cost of delivering data is on the order of 100 times too expensive for this to be economically feasible yet. The cost of subsidizing even basic services for free would exceed many people's monthly income and it would be extremely difficult for the industry to build a profitable model. However, with an organized effort, we think it is reasonable to expect the overall efficiency of delivering data to increase by 100x in the next 5–10 years."[25]

You might say I was focused in the first two chapters on professions dominated by men. Actually, they have plenty of women, but I have been remiss to have not focused on female workers in those chapters. Let's rectify that in the next chapter.

---

[25] https://www.facebook.com/isconnectivityahumanright

CHAPTER 3

The Female of the Species

⌇→

Women were scarce in the first two chapters, but in many ways, they are changing several professions with technological applications. Let's start with public accounting.

Digitizing Digits

Franciscan friars may be associated with beer brewing, but one of them, Fra Luca Pacioli, is jokingly referred to as the patron saint of IRS auditors. Pacioli first described double-entry bookkeeping in 1494. It's still a bedrock principle in modern accounting.

Meanwhile, when I started my career at Price Waterhouse in the 1980s as a hotshot MBA, I wanted to be part of the firm's systems consulting group. They advised me to go through the audit ranks and learn about business processes at large companies as a good grounding for the systems work. I did so—grudgingly—and learned that the auditing profession was paper- and labor-intensive. This was before the days of laptops and bar codes on assets, and I did more than my fair share of inventory counts in grimy factories and grain silos, plus stuffing envelopes with typewritten confirmation letters to banks. I actually looked forward to the inventory counts since they took me to new places and away from the tedium of paperwork. There were many days that I thought the accounting profession had evolved little in the centuries since the good friar first wrote about bookkeeping. I jumped at the first opportunity to move over to the consulting side.

The audit profession has evolved considerably in the three decades since. Most clients now conduct their transactions in ERP systems, and their biggest worry is digital breaches. Regulators like the U.S. SEC expect reporting in XBRL and other digital formats. Many auditors leverage sites like Confirmation.com to digitize the letters I used to stuff.

If two women in New York City have their way, that pace of technological automation in the accounting profession will accelerate in the next few years.

Amy Pawlicki is Director of Business Reporting, Assurance and Advisory Services which she describes as "the Reporting and Assurance Services R&D team" of the American Institute of CPAs (AICPA).

In an interview, she told me:

> "Half of what my group focuses on from an assurance perspective is the innovation of the traditional financial statement audit. That's something that has really ramped up in the last couple of years. The AICPA Assurance Services Executive Committee and Auditing Standards Board have spent a significant amount of time deliberating over the past five years or so to lay the groundwork for the transition that we now see starting to materialize. These two committees are now collaborating on the development of professional guidance on the use of analytics and automation in the traditional financial statement audit.
>
> The reality is that today's standards don't preclude the use of analytics and automation, but they were written at a time when it wasn't possible. They call for things to be done, like sampling or manual checks, in situations where today you could do 100% validation or can check something with much greater accuracy electronically than you could with a physical on-site visit and in a much more timely and efficient

manner. Even though the standards don't prevent the use of analytics or automation in the audit, they don't encourage it. Practitioners may still feel hesitant to substitute new approaches in situations where a more traditional approach, like sampling, is explicitly referenced in the standards.

As mentioned earlier, we are in the process of updating and expanding our current Analytical Procedures Guide into a new Audit Analytics Guide slated for release in 2017. We're starting with a guide at the foundational level that will be relevant to firms of all sizes, because we don't think that the benefits of automation and analytics are in any way limited to large firms. You don't need sophisticated software programs, either. You can use Excel for most of what we're building into this initial iteration of the guide.

Version two of the guide is where we would get into more advanced analytics. When I say advanced, I'm talking about really cool stuff like machine learning, artificial intelligence, textual analytics, and process mining. We have a very long list of topics that we want to explore. To learn more about what the future of audit might look like, you may want to check out the free compendium of essays that AICPA published entitled Audit Analytics and Continuous Audit, Looking Toward the Future.[26] This compendium includes contributions from Professors and PhD students from Rutgers Business School, as well as a number of professionals who participate in their research, and has been very well received."

She mentions that all of the larger accounting firms are developing and using very innovative tools. One example that has received accolades is Deloitte's tool, called Argus, that can automatically identify and extract key accounting information from any type of electronic document. It has been used to parse information

---

[26] http://www.aicpa.org/InterestAreas/FRC/AssuranceAdvisoryServices/
DownloadableDocuments/AuditAnalytics_LookingTowardFuture.pdf

on tens of thousands of sales, leasing, and derivatives contracts, employment agreements, invoices, client meeting minutes, legal letters, and financial statements. Deloitte also has an in-memory data analytics engine called Optix that its auditors can use in real time to analyze vast populations of data.

Shaun Budnik is the Audit Innovation leader at another large firm, KPMG LLP (KPMG). Her group brings together the technologies, analytic techniques, and processes to develop "audit and assurance services of the future." Prior to this, she played a similar role at Deloitte and also focused on educational programming that has had a significant impact on the profession.

KPMG recently announced an agreement with IBM, allowing it to apply IBM's Watson cognitive computing technology to many of KPMG's services. Even though financial reporting is about numbers, audits tend to involve scores of judgment calls about internal controls, reviews of contracts, accuracy of statements, and other risk-based assessments.

Budnik told me in an interview, "It's what we're calling at this point a supervised technology. Artificial intelligence can take all the variables you use to make a judgment and it makes the same judgment faster, with ultimately more precision."[27] IBM's view: "Auditing and similar knowledge services are increasingly challenged with tackling immense volumes of unstructured data. Cognitive technologies such as Watson can transform how this data is understood and how critical decisions are made."[28]

Said Budnik:

> "We are barely scratching the surface when you talk unstructured data. For instance, take a scenario where you have video cameras in your receiving and shipping ports. You

---

[27] KPMG LLP requested we add this disclaimer "This content represents the views of the author(s) only, and does not necessarily represent the views or professional advice of KPMG LLP."

[28] http://www.prnewswire.com/news-releases/kpmg-announces-agreement-with-ibm-watson-to-help-deliver-cognitive-powered-insights-300231890.html

are able to see visually when packages leave and when they arrive. You could translate that unstructured data and compare it to actual shipping and receiving data that people are entering in the computer. Or you might leverage RFID in the warehouse to track those items. There's so much more technology available to converge with cognitive tools."

Could some disruptive external player create the audit of the future? Pawlicki weighed in: "Public company audits have to be performed by a licensed CPA. From that perspective, we have unique training and expertise, not to mention extensive requirements for adhering to professional standards and a code of ethics, all of which reinforces our strength and credibility as a profession, but I don't think that's a license for complacency. We need to continue to leverage technology and information toward innovation that improves the quality of audits and the relevance of all other services we perform as a profession."

There is another debate in this profession which has historically used sophisticated sampling in its reviews. Said Budnik, "I think the regulators will need to ask, 'Does the fact that technology provides us with more things to audit mean we have to audit them?' Is there an expectation that because we *can* now audit 100% that we *should* audit 100%?"

That is prompting debates about "continuous audits." According to Budnik, "When you start bringing in lightning-fast, in-memory technologies, can you have them do those judgment-based tasks on a more frequent basis, maybe even daily? If you're looking at contracts or loans, every time a loan is generated in a bank, can you have that loan go through the cognitive process of being reviewed, inspected, and analyzed?"

Budnik explained another complexity:

"We're used to getting paper from clients as a source of their transactions. Now you obtain a data file. We have to validate independently all the controls over the data—how they flow, how they're processed and how they're approved—before we can even ingest the data and do our own analysis on them. That's been a big hurdle for many of us—understanding that cleansing process, as well as understanding the data flow. The number of specialists and techies needed to really understand that has skyrocketed."

And this shift is changing the talent needs of the profession.

Budnik said, "KPMG recognizes that in the future our professionals will need a broader educational background and mix of abilities. Specifically, graduates coming into the profession will need analytical skills and a much deeper understanding of technology and its uses in financial reporting and auditing. In fact, I believe we'll see extended audit teams that will be composed of a variety of professionals and include accountants, data scientists, computer engineers, and financial analysts."

Pawlicki added, "AICPA has partnered with Rutgers to create a new initiative called RADAR, which is an acronym for Rutgers AICPA Data Analytics Research Initiative. Eight of the largest accounting firms are engaged in that initiative to start doing foundational research around key areas that we think are most important to support the application of our guidance and practice by firms of all sizes."

Both Pawlicki and Budnik are poised to have front row seats watching the torrent of changes coming to the accounting profession.

Ads Infinitum

Elsewhere in Manhattan, Julie Bauer has been at the forefront of another profession which has embraced digital change, somewhat more than accounting. Bauer is cofounder of the digital advertising agency, Grok. She cut her teeth at large agencies like Ogilvy & Mather and Saatchi & Saatchi, but is a geek at heart. She holds on to her Commodore 64, the 8-bit home computer that she helped launch in 1982. She calls the "1984" Apple commercial the most memorable one she has seen in her long career: "One commercial and one airing changed everything." About her firm's name, she says, "Grok is a term that only scientists, engineers, and sci-fi freaks use, but we love the word and what it stands for." [The dictionary definition is "to understand something profoundly and intuitively." Robert Heinlein coined the word in his classic sci-fi book, *Stranger in a Strange Land*.]

I asked her about how the advertising world has changed with digital technologies.

> "In the past, in the creative department you would have an art director and a copywriter. They functioned as a team; they came up with an idea and then that idea got farmed out to a production outfit. Today, if you're not doing digital production within your agency, you're missing out on probably one of the biggest revenue generators. Seven or eight years ago when we started, we had no capacity to do anything digital within the agency. I would say today 50% of our creative staff is what we call creative coders. They understand how to code. They understand how to produce digital work, but they also come out of art school or come out of a creative background. If you want to produce a video they know how to do it in-house. We took a back conference room in our little agency and soundproofed it so that we can make videos. For a small agency like ours, it's been a fairly easy transition—we were able to shift much quicker and much easier than the big, cumbersome, larger agencies.
>
> I think from a creative standpoint, when I see what some of my creative guys, what they can do on their computer, it just blows my mind. If I say it would be cool if we could do this and my one art director, who is Brazilian, will look at me and say, 'I can do that, Julie.'
>
> Look at Hollywood, and how computer generated imagery (CGI) has changed filmmaking. There is obviously big

budget CGI, and then there is the ability to do almost any-thing that mimics the effects of CGI on a Mac. We will see less and less live action filming because it is expensive. You have to go on location. You have to blow up a bunch of cars. Instead, you can blow up a bunch of cars on a computer. But you can tell the difference. See how much TV today is low-production-value reality TV. It's dirt cheap to produce. Then you see something like *House of Cards* come along and people flock to it because people appreciate the production value. I think there's a balance. There's a time and place for everything. You would hate to see the artistry of true creative talent go unappreciated in the future.

Think of the latest episode of *Star Wars*. Without J.J. Abrams having some kind of a vision on how to make that story, tell that story, it could have been an awful movie. Now, granted, he's got a lot more machines at his disposal and he's got a lot more ways of producing stuff, but that vision and that creativity will hopefully never go away.

I have a client which competes with Procter & Gamble. Part of our value is to help them think about what P&G will do, and how not to react. We're going to be smarter, we're going to work on a smaller budget. At the end of the day, a machine cannot replace the creativity of the human brain. I think that the machine, that the technology out there, complements it and makes it easier for creative people to do more interesting things.

Having said that, there are clients that want to move everything to digital advertising. If it cannot be measured down to the penny then they don't want to bother with it. I caution our clients that the world has not changed that much. Yes, a person may click on a banner but who knows whether they clicked at it because they happened to see your advertising at the airport and thought, 'Hmm, that looks interesting to me.' Then they happen to be sitting on a plane and saw your ad in a magazine and finally they turn on their computer and they saw your ad again and decided, 'Yeah, now I should click on this and see what else I can find.'

Working through multiple channels is still important. You want them to see what happens in China. In China, billboards work, digital works, and print works. All of them work. It's because it's all new. People there are not jaded—they're hungry to see more and learn more.

I do think we have to learn as a profession that we have to work smarter and quicker. It reflects our clients and their need for speed to market, especially with technology clients. Clients can't afford to overthink things. They have to get things out because technology constantly forces their products to also be changing. That's a huge shift in our profession.

We also have to accept that business models have changed dramatically. Clients don't want to pay for usage. A photographer can't go to my client and say I want you to spend $50,000 or $100,000 to do a shoot but you can't put it on your website. In the past, photographers made all their money on royalty. Today you can't stop where the images are used. If I shoot a commercial for them, they will want to put the video on their website and they will want to have it on YouTube. There's no way they want to pay talent usage fees. They buy the images outright, and that's just a totally different mentality where people need to rethink the way they make money. At the end of the day what technology is doing is forcing our industry to rethink its business model."

Marketing Payback

Nearly a century ago, department store pioneer John Wanamaker lamented that half his marketing budget was a waste. He just wished he could figure out which half. Wanamaker could have used the services of Heidi Melin, the Chief Marketing Officer at Plex Systems, and Jennifer Pockell Dimas, Melin's "digital guru."

Melin and Pockell Dimas represent the new face of marketing complex products such as the manufacturing software that Plex develops.

Said Melin:

> "Today, we can essentially measure everything that results from a dollar being invested in marketing. Earlier in my career [in her role at an advertising agency], I would easily spend millions of dollars of my client's money with zero accountability. We'd run an ad in a print publication or on broadcast and you thought perhaps it had an impact on the brand, and you'd measure that impact maybe once a year. Don't get me wrong—it was fun; but it was a little more, I like to say, about arts and crafts because it was about making things look beautiful, capturing people's attention, and creating an image. That's fun. We still have that but today everything is automated and we're able to match that investment to revenue. We knew marketing had an influence, but we just knew that intuitively and we couldn't prove it. Today, with digital, we're able to measure the impact of every dollar that we invest.
>
> Our goal is to give our sales people granular information on every customer—visitors to the website, what they've downloaded, which parts of the website they visited, what campaigns they have responded to, where they raised their hand for more information. That's the kind of stuff that becomes so valuable in the relationship—they can have a much better informed conversation with the customer and create a more valuable exchange in the selling conversation than they've ever been able to have before."

Pockell Dimas, who has more of a technical than an "arts and crafts" background, explained some of the marketing technologies they use:

> "We use Adobe as our web and asset management platform, and Eloqua for email and other campaigns. The leads from both are summarized into Salesforce Sales Cloud. Once the deal closes in Salesforce, it's passed along to the services portion of our consulting group [which may also be a partner] for implementation. When the customer is live, they work with our support team using the Salesforce Service Cloud. We also use Jive as our community platform.
>
> And then we use plenty of specialist tools like Oceanos for contact list building and enrichment, Demandbase to personalize customer outreach, Vidyard for video marketing, Kapost for content management, and many others."

Melin said her firm's commitment to accountability is exemplified by a dashboard she constantly monitors and presents regularly to her CEO and Board.

One of the dashboard's metrics is Volume of Media Coverage which might read like this:

> "In Q3, we secured 48 pieces of earned coverage in publications including *Forbes, IndustryWeek, TechCrunch, ComputerWorld, Deal Architect, Diginomica,* and *Techonomy.* The State of Manufacturing Technology report continued its momentum and received pick up on other tech-focused and manufacturing blogs. In addition, Plex secured 18 pieces of placed coverage, and was published on Industryweek.com, CIO.com, Diginomica.com, and Plex.com."

Another key metric is Social Impressions:

> "Our social media efforts this quarter resulted in 513K organic impressions on LinkedIn and Twitter, a 19% increase from Q2. The new baseline for Q4 will be 512K impressions."

Pockell Dimas summarized the marketing unit's charter:

> "It's like when you walk into a store. When the salesperson comes up to you and can tell you're looking for something specific, they help you out and they save you time, plus you've established a personal relationship. And then there's the salesperson who does not watch your cues, who is so irritating that you just want to leave the store. We are here to give our sales force all the digital cues they need to better understand their customers."

Edifice Complex

Across the pond, Prince Charles has often expressed strong opinions on modern architecture. As he has commented, "I have lost count of the times I have been accused of wanting to turn the clock back to some Golden Age. Nothing could be further from my mind. My concern is the future."[29] He points to the need for the architecture profession to balance inspiration from the past and from nature with the experimental capabilities that advances in CAD, 3-D printing, and material science afford. Zaha Hadid was just such an architect who was pushing the boundaries of those advances.

Till her untimely passing in March 2016, Hadid was the lead partner of her London firm that has architected dazzling structures around the world. Her senior partner, Patrik Schumacher, has called their work "parametricism," which he views as "a successor

---

[29] http://www.independent.co.uk/arts-entertainment/architecture/prince-charles-discovers-10-ways-to-antagonise-architects-with-list-of-geometric-principles-9939013.html

to postmodernism: shaping architecture with algorithms, computer design, and new materials."[30]

Hadid's first major commission was the Vitra Fire Station in Germany, distinctive with its hard concrete structural bends. Her toughest assignment, she had said, was the MAXXI Italian National Museum of the 21st Century Arts in Rome, which took a decade to construct and has been hailed as a masterpiece by critics. More successes followed, including the Aquatics Center for the 2012 London Olympics and the Guangzhou Opera House.

Hadid was quoted in an interview:

> "Our designs become more ambitious as we see the new possibilities created by the technology of other industries. There is a strong reciprocal relationship whereby our more ambitious design visions encourage the continuing development of the new digital technologies and fabrication techniques, and those new developments in turn inspire us to push the design envelope ever further. The current state of architecture and design requires extensive collaboration and an investigative attitude, and we continue to research and develop new technologies."[31]

Hadid fought multiple biases—as a woman in her profession and as an immigrant to the UK (she was born in Iraq)—to become one of the most highly recognized architects in the world. She was the first woman to receive the Pritzker Architecture Prize, and the first woman to receive a Gold Medal from the Royal Institute of British Architects. Critics have praised her work for its "structural pyrotechnics," "bold curves," and "free flowing fluidity."

---

[30] http://mobile.nytimes.com/2016/04/21/arts/design/grieving-and-going-forward-how-zaha-hadids-firm-plans-to-moveon.html?emc=edit_th_20160421&nl=todays headlines&nlid=47889359&_r=0&referer=

[31] http://www.designboom.com/architecture/zaha-hadid-interview-quotes-dies-aged-65-03-31-2016/

Beyond grand buildings, she also tried her hand at product design. In her words:

> "There is a lot of fluidity now between art, architecture, and fashion—a lot more cross-pollination in the disciplines—but this isn't about competition, it's about collaboration and what these practices and processes can contribute to one another."

In an obituary for her, *Architect* magazine described Hadid's wider work:

> "Her ever-growing portfolio (her studio announced an accessories line with Georg Jensen last week) includes jewelry, vessels, seating, a prototype car, and more than a few shoes, all of which confer the sinuous, sculptural, and whimsical nature of her award-winning structures at a scale that makes them tangible, even personal."[32]

Meanwhile, at the construction sites, robots are turning ambitious new designs into reality. A masonry robot called SAM can lay bricks. Another robot called Thor can scoop piles of dirt and load it into the back of a truck. And in Switzerland, flying bots are being trained to weave ropes together to make a bridge.

With her "starchitect" image Hadid also drew controversy, and her work in Japan, Qatar, and China drew criticism. Nonetheless, she will continue to inspire architects to take advantage of technological advances.

Quantifying Organizational Behavior

Nina Kohli-Laven is a global citizen who grew up in San Francisco and London. She studied anthropology at the University of Michigan and her dissertation research focused on the politics

---

[32] http://www.architectmagazine.com/technology/products/the-product-design-of-zaha-hadid_o

of history-making in New France, French North America, and Quebec. In her professional life, Kohli-Laven has researched a variety of topics in a wide range of institutions. She analyzes organizational behavior at McKinsey, and in previous roles did country risk analysis for IHS in Singapore, and economic analytics at Altusys.

It is fascinating to hear her discuss how anthropologists, diplomats, and strategy consultants around the world are evolving as they work with the latest technology:

> "At Altusys, we built situational awareness tools using mobile technologies for field operations in health, finance, and government. I worked on a tool called Provisional Economic Analysis that is Rapid and Local (PEARL), which was designed for field workers in humanitarian, development, and other emergency response operations. The tool helped field workers make quick decisions about how to act based on incomplete or uncertain data. We found that with the tool's aid, NGOs in the field were collecting more information to form well-grounded intuitions. We would collect casual measures like observations and opinions about key grievances. We could ask, 'Are young men at home, are they working and, if they are not home, how long they are gone for?' We could quantify, for example, how polarized a community was along tribal lines.
>
> At McKinsey, in the OrgSolutions group, we are essentially trying to achieve the same thing: the creation of standard, numerical frameworks for describing human behavior, in order to push those frameworks into software tools that can then be used by nonexperts to "diagnose" behavioral groups (in our case, companies and public sector organizations).
>
> Coaches, psychologists, organizational change practitioners, and a range of other consultants have been helping companies define cultural strengths and weaknesses

for decades. You could call it the "organizational change" industry, and it's always been driven by consultants/experts who do very bespoke, project-based work. The key questions guiding what we do here are, 'Can you distill that expertise?', 'Can you codify it in a way that applies across cases?', and 'Can you embed that codification in software that delivers a meaningful set of insights and recommendations?' And one of the ongoing questions in this kind of work, a very practical question, is, 'How do we develop insights that are sufficiently customized to speak to the client's needs, but that don't deviate from the standard solution (software, service delivery, etc.) so much that we can't scale?'

Scaling in a strategy consulting firm is the real conundrum. On the one hand, you've got an imperative to serve clients, many of whom have unique needs and demand unique service. In most (but not all) consulting organizations, you've got a mind-set, honed over years, that the client comes first. Which translates into attending to the unique demands of each particular client. This precludes the creation of standard offerings that can be delivered at higher volume with similar levels of effort. On the other hand, you've got this very lucrative possibility of developing a standardized approach that may serve 60% or 80% of the client's needs, and that we can deliver on a much more cost-effective basis.

At IHS, I worked in the services arm of a data product company. It was the opposite of my role at McKinsey, where I am in the product arm of a services company. In the services group at IHS, our client work was always custom and often highly tailored to individual clients. We used proprietary economic data to help build custom market forecasts for clients. For instance, for a large mining client we developed an online tool they could use to track and score key economic and political indicators on the future market opportunity for raw minerals in 15 different countries."

Automation on the Syllabus

In Chapter 1 we met Mihir Shukla, the CEO of Automation Anywhere. His former COO (ex-Sun Microsystems and PwC), Kathleen Holmgren, is now tasked at the company with influencing educational curricula for adapting to the coming wave of robotic process automation (RPA). Operating under the idea that if you want to change the future of work you have to also change the future workforce, Holmgren has already been influential in the educational realm, having served on the advisory board at the Stanford Graduate School of Business, and she is currently sitting as a board member at California Polytechnic State University, San Luis Obispo, CA, College of Engineering.

As Holmgren relayed to me:

> "My role with Mihir and the company is to figure out how we can assist universities in embedding robotic process automation concepts into their curriculum. We are putting together a comprehensive certification program at the moment, and plan to roll it out later this year. In support of these efforts, I spoke this past month at the National Convention of Industrial Engineers and met with both IE professionals as well as several university department chairs on the growing influence that the field of RPA will have on their students and their curricula.
>
> I believe the industrial engineering curriculum offers a significant opportunity for developing and incorporating RPA education. IEs are chartered in most organizations to improve operational efficiency, quality, and productivity. Therefore, RPA needs to be a part of the graduating IE's tool bag. Computer software engineering coursework is another obvious choice. Even in business curricula: What will be the extent of business function automation? What will be the effect of implemented automation processes— when and where is it appropriate to use it? All are concepts

that should be discussed and included in these learning environments.

We are having ongoing conversations right now with several universities regarding the role of automation education as a key element in preparing our future professionals. Our goal is to help them find the best way in which Automation Anywhere can help them incorporate RPA into their curriculum. Ideas being discussed include having our personnel teach a class or become a visiting lecturer for a few days to introduce the concepts. We are just at the beginning stages of our educational institution effort. I was the COO of Automation Anywhere till October of 2015, so this development program is a relatively new position for me, and I'm just starting to make contacts with the universities, finding out how we can help, and determining how we can best offer our knowledge and skill set to them and their students.

One of the other avenues that we're pursuing is working with adult education institutes like an IIT in India and others in the U.S. These focus on skill-based training and certification for people who want to enhance their existing skill sets or reskill themselves for a different career. It's possible that India is where we're going to start, because this market is very receptive and ready for RPA due to the large number of business process outsourcing (BPO) companies. These businesses are now looking for and hiring RPA-skilled talent. Given the budgeting process at most U.S. public universities, it often takes longer to change the curriculum and add new areas of study. Therefore, it is likely we will be able to make inroads happen quicker in India, and work concurrently within the U.S. to make it a significant area of study as soon as possible. RPA is a global certainty at some point in the future, as evidenced by our conversations with institutions in Europe which have also expressed interest in RPA certification programs."

Holmgren may just be getting started, but her efforts are already paying off. RPA from her company and those of Blue Prism and UIpath, among others, are hot topics in most outsourcing firms. Given that many focus on white-collar processes in industries like banking, insurance, and health care, it is RPA—more than autonomous cars, drones, and other forms of automation—that is getting more of their attention.

Women, men, white collar, blue collar . . . almost every job is being reshaped by technology. Now you could say that these are all in global, tech-savvy places with sophisticated employers like McKinsey. Let's look at jobs in the far less tech-savvy part of Florida where I currently live.

CHAPTER 4

The Internet of Humble Jobs

⌇→

We live in what my Irish wife calls Paradise on the west coast of Florida. She adores the weather, even with our hurricanes and the fact that we are the lightning capital of the world with over a million strikes a year. I like it here, too, partly because a very efficient airport, 10 minutes away, allows me to fly nonstop to over 50 cities around the world.

The Big Guava

Besides, I love the fact that my office is under a shady oak tree with a Buddha watching over me, with mullets jumping out of the water in the canal, and squirrels, cardinals, and blue jays coming to visit all day long. Granted, they come for the bird seed, but it breaks the monotony of the office.

Our baseball team is in the same division as the New York Yankees. The Big Guava vs. The Big Apple is not a fair battle. Our paradise does not win many high-tech battles, either. We are known here for cigars and Cuban sandwiches, not computer chips. Yet, even in Tampa Bay, we see plenty of "silicon collars" and tech-savvy consumers.

Take my neighbor Keith Gallops, who pretends to be a tech novice and asks tongue in cheek, "Are algorithms named after Al Gore since he invented the internet?" He is savvy enough to email Zillow, the real estate site, about a dispute related to the value of his house. He showed me what he wrote them: "If you really believe you do not have a way to manually update or edit the Zestimate algorithm, then my little problem pales in comparison to yours." Gallops was convinced he was dealing with a Zillow bot. I told him to double check that she was not Amy Irving, the bot who helps schedule meetings courtesy of the start-up X.ai (her initials cleverly share the acronym for Artificial Intelligence). As it turned out, she was not a bot. A couple of months later, his house's value was up considerably, so the human agent likely overrode the algorithm.

Trash Talk

Let's look at garbage collection in our neighborhood. Our county has 95-gallon garbage bins with sensors which allow for easy verification if a street has not been serviced. They are emptied into garbage trucks equipped with McNeilus AutoReach robotic arms.

Amaury, the driver, operates a Republic Services truck, and he visits our street twice a week. He operates the robotic arm from the cab of his truck. In a full day he can gather over 1,200 bins, twice as many as he previously did with a human partner. Amaury no longer needs the associate dangling at the back of the truck doing a dangerous and stinky job. The contribution of the robotic arm: half the human resources, twice the production, and a much less tiring job.

Our county claims this automation has brought other benefits, such as keeping the neighborhoods cleaner and neater. Prior to this, each household used their own style of garbage "bin," and many just left bags out. It also increases recycle rates and related revenues, which keep our fees down.

The Volvo Group is planning to take such garbage collection into narrower streets and to places where the weather is not as pleasant as in my Florida county. Its Robot-based Autonomous Refuse (ROAR) project entails much more than a truck with a robotic arm. A robot carried at the back of the truck will zip around the streets and bring the garbage bins to the truck. A drone launched from the truck's roof will scan the area and guide the robot to the bins.

The garbage bin itself is evolving and will further change the collection of garbage. BigBelly makes solar-powered trash compactors, which can hold eight times more garbage than a standard bin. Volume sensors trigger the compacting mechanism and the bin communicates with a cloud-based management system which coordinates collections. Since collections can be done on an as-needed basis, it will streamline collections. The company says there are other benefits—CO_2 emissions are reduced and neighborhoods are much tidier.

The Brown Collar

Let's next meet Ken, the UPS deliveryman for our neighborhood. For over two decades, he has had a constant companion: The Delivery Information Acquisition Device (DIAD), which guides delivery routes, gets delivery confirmations from customers, and helps the drivers in many other ways. Without DIADs, it is highly unlikely UPS could deliver over 35 million packages a day during the peak holiday season.

DIAD was developed for UPS in the late 1980s by Motorola, and first deployed in 1990, before the iPhone or the iPad were even conceived. Its battery lasts all day—much longer than the batteries in most Apple or Android devices. Now in its fifth generation, it can communicate with both CDMA and GPRS cellular technologies to stay connected with multiple carriers. The DIAD V has features such as a camera, dimensional imaging, wireless LAN capabilities, touch screen and keypad, more memory, and faster CPU, and is approximately half the size and weight of its predecessor, the DIAD IV.

Over the decades, DIAD has allowed UPS to capture billions of data points on addresses, routes, and driver tendencies. This has allowed UPS to develop its On-Road Integrated Optimization and Navigation (ORION) to ensure its drivers use the most optimized delivery routes with regard to distance, fuel, and time. UPS describes it, "Arguably the world's largest operations research project, ORION uses expansive fleet telematics and advanced algorithms to gather and calculate countless amounts of data to provide UPS drivers with optimized routes. The technology helps UPS drivers to determine the optimal way to deliver and pick up packages within a set of stops defined by start time, commit time, pick-up windows and special customer needs."[33]

Sensors on the UPS truck track engine performance and simulate what the driver does all week long. That data has led to reductions in excessive idling, and the now-famous UPS "no left turns" dictum on the majority of their routes (to reduce time, fuel, and accidents). It has also allowed UPS to reduce reversing occurrences by a quarter. One mile per driver per day over one year can save UPS up to $50 million in fuel costs. One minute of time saved per driver is worth half a million dollars a year to UPS, so the technologies have made them highly productive workers. They are also much safer drivers, as they log nearly three billion miles per year with less than one accident per million miles driven. UPS inducts drivers who have 25 years of incident-free driving into its "Circle of Honor." In 2016, 8,700 drivers had reached that milestone.[34]

Raising the Roof

More on our street: my wife and I dreaded getting our house reroofed. We had visions of days of chaos and being exposed to the elements. Then I saw a neighbor's roof transformed overnight—almost as if someone had sprinkled pixie dust while they were sleeping. So we took the plunge, and I was impressed at the automation and efficiency of the process.

It started with a truck equipped with a conveyor belt which rapidly moved shingles and other materials to the top of the roof.

---

[33] https://www.pressroom.ups.com/pressroom/ContentDetailsViewer.page?ConceptType=Factsheets&id=1426321616277-282

[34] https://pressroom.ups.com/pressroom/ContentDetailsViewer.page?ConceptType=PressReleases&id=1456259160760-389

A crew stripped off the old roof and tossed the materials into another truck, which took the stuff to be recycled.

The modern roofer works with a Stanley staple gun, wears Cougar Paw shoes which help keep him from sliding on debris on sloping roofs, and uses Husky magnetic sweepers to keep the work site tidy. Our contractor, Magyar Roofing, diligently documented every step of the way with over 90 images on digital camera.

The humble shingle is designed these days for aesthetics, energy efficiency, and algae resistance. Also, and importantly for us in Florida, they are meant to handle winds up to 130 mph that accompany some hurricanes. It's not just the shingles—there are layers of moisture barrier, undereave ventilation, and insulation that supplement the shingle protection.

As I said, I was impressed. The Magyar crew did the work over two days, and could have squeezed the job into one day if we did not have a two-tiered roof. A couple of decades ago, that work took much longer, was much less safe, and was not nearly as well documented.

The digital documentation that the contractor provided us and the inspection they arranged also helped us get a significant discount on our home insurance. Pixie dust, indeed.

Never Run Out of Juice

Our backyard used to have several citrus trees. A blight called citrus greening has been afflicting the trees throughout the state. When we had the trees, the fresh orange juice was exquisite, but it was an effort to harvest the fruit with a 10 foot picker, to squeeze the fruit, and get rid of the rotting skins. So every time I come across a Tropicana carton outside the U.S., I admire the marvel of producing the juice at massive scale.

The supply chains for Tropicana (owned by Pepsi-Cola in nearby Bradenton) and Simply (owned by Coca-Cola in Auburndale) orange juice provide a glimpse of the automation needed to produce juice and illustrate how jobs in the industry have evolved.

Larger orange groves utilize robotic harvesters. The Oxbo tree shakers and pickup equipment can work day and night and collect up to a million pounds of fruit a day. Frost, which can be deadly to the crop, is easier to monitor with today's sensors. Satellite imagery is used these days to optimize picking times.

Then you get into the processing, and the steps there would humble most brewmasters—getting the aroma, color, and taste just right; the flash pasteurization; and the handling of all the by-products (including using the peel to create a form of ethanol). Next is the state-of-the-art packaging, and finally shipping, via pipeline, refrigerated rail cars, and shipping containers.

Coca-Cola uses what it calls its Black Book to optimize the production process. From *BusinessWeek*:

> "The Black Book model includes detailed data about the myriad flavors—more than 600 in all—that make up an orange, and consumer preferences. Those data are matched to a profile detailing acidity, sweetness, and other attributes of each batch of raw juice. The algorithm then tells Coke how to blend batches to replicate a certain taste and consistency, right down to pulp content. Another part of Black Book incorporates external factors such as weather patterns, expected crop yields, and cost pressures. This helps Coke plan so that supplies will be on hand as far ahead as 15 months."[35]

In Chapter 1, Tyler Scheid commented on how he saw his vineyard as a manufacturing plant. "It just happens to use solar radiation as input, but it's essentially a factory," he said. Next time you enjoy some juice, think of the complex "plant" which

---

[35] http://www.bloomberg.com/news/articles/2013-01-31/coke-engineers-its-orange-juice-with-an-algorithm

manufactures it. Now, let's look at more farm products—the food in restaurants and the technology which surrounds it.

Comfort Food

Talking of farms, in nearby Dade City—which is famous for another citrus variety called the tart kumquat—Curtis Beebe runs a restaurant called Pearl in the Grove. He could easily position it within the "farm to table" genre, but he prefers the humbler "home cooking" moniker. The rave reviews inform us that it does not matter how you classify it.

He has a unique background for a chef/owner:

> "I spent over 25 years as a technology consultant, on the road much of that time, eating in restaurants and observing and learning what worked well and what didn't. Then when the time came to shift gears from a career standpoint, that experience, coupled with a pretty deep family background in terms of food, especially Southern regional cuisine . . . it just kind of seemed like a natural progression for us. We opened our little fine dining place five-and-a-half years ago, and heard from folks they also wanted a more casual place. So we opened a gastropub, the Local Public House, two years ago, and then a year ago we opened our neighborhood bistro called Rebecca's [named after his wife].
>
> My IT career has given me a couple of interesting perspectives on this business. Few of my chef/owner peers have seen the insides of as many restaurants as I had during my consulting travel. They are also pretty conservative in terms of technology—they are afraid of it being both a cost and a time sink trying to make it work. I am more willing to try out different technologies."

Beebe discussed a number of technologies that are transforming his labor-intensive industry. He also pointed out that one size does *not* fit all across his three establishments:

"The single technology that has had the most impact on the business is social media. We wouldn't have even been able to launch the first restaurant without social media. I don't think there would have been any other way to reach our potential customers without it. Print wouldn't work. Broadcast media would have been too expensive for us.

In terms of customer-facing business apps, the most useful one is OpenTable. There are two components to that—the reservation management component and, more importantly for us, the marketing component. OpenTable has so many users that whenever somebody is looking for a restaurant, that's the first place they go. Being on that list has been pretty important to us. It lets us plan seatings more efficiently and it gives us good recurring customer data, where we can make a note that Mrs. Jones is a vegetarian, so let's make sure we have a nice vegetable entrée on her next visit. Today is Ed's birthday or anniversary, so let's customize the service accordingly. However, ours is not a very high margin business, OpenTable is not that cheap, and we still get a fair number of reservations by phone. So we use a much less expensive reservation management application called DineTime at Rebecca's. It helps with our scheduling but does not have the marketing functionality of OpenTable.

We use Constant Contact for our email management system and use their EventSpot feature for selling tickets for special events. We use the NCR Aloha point-of-sale system at the gastropub. That includes wireless, handheld devices and wireless printers. They format customer orders and print them in the kitchen, and provide us visibility on what we're selling, typical ticket turn times, and other data. Aloha also has an app called Pulse. I can look on my phone and tell you how many hamburgers we've sold, how many returns we've had that may have been due to quality or just misordering, who's clocked in, who isn't, what our labor-to-revenue ratio is. That allows me to run the place without being there as much. It's a management-labor-saving device.

In reverse, we continue with a cash register at the Pearl. I don't think the efficiencies would warrant the point-of-sale system there. We have 15 tables, and 40 handwritten tickets an evening is manageable.

We use a staff scheduling app called ScheduleFly, where my managers make template schedules and publish them for the staff. In turn, staff can adjust the schedules if they need to take a night off or give up a shift. They can give it up online and somebody else can pick it up without any management intervention, which is pretty effective for us.

Recipe management is still old school. We have a shared Google Drive folder for each place, with our menus and recipes, so everyone in the kitchens has access to it that way. For menu management, on the other hand, we use SinglePlatform. That allows us to format the menu electronically and distribute it to multiple sites. We just send it to them in either a PDF or a Word document and they convert it. They have a plug-in for our websites. Those menus also get picked up by many of the social media and review sites. If you go to TripAdvisor and say 'view menu,' it's actually using the SinglePlatform plug-in to display the menu.

Not all the technologies we try pan out. There's a cultural thing in our business—customers are uncomfortable shelling out the tip and signing the slip while the server stands there. So we have a portable Bluetooth printer where the server can swipe the card, print the slip, and bring it to the customer—and come back and pick it up later. I was hoping to get away from credit card slips, but I am not sure we will get there.

One technology which was a complete nonstarter was Aloha's Mobile Pay application. It allows customers to pay their check via their phone. The check would print with a unique QR code. The customer would scan the QR code with their phone, and their check would come up, and they could order other items and it would update. Then they could use PayPal or a stored credit card. Customers were just not interested in the service. We pushed that mobile payment service for a year and when we turned it off, we didn't hear a peep out of anybody."

It is fair to say that as Apple Pay and other mobile payment methods evolve, Beebe will continue to experiment with technology as he does his menus, and his employees will continue to be some of the most tech-savvy in the business.

The Most Tech-Savvy Retail Store?

Let's next go half a mile down the road to our neighborhood Home Depot. When you think of technology in stores, you think of the Apple Genius Bar, the Best Buy Geek Squad, or the Tesla associate who walks around with an iPad. Don't laugh, but the Home Depot associate is actually surrounded by a huge amount of technology. She is supported by the company's 1,500 miles of data/fiber cable. Big as the store is, you can order another half a million items online. It's fair to say a Home Depot associate sees a lot more than just lumber and plumbing fixtures on a daily basis, and many of the items are endowed with ZigBee and Bluetooth.

I usually scan for an item on the Home Depot mobile app as I enter the store, and it tells me the exact aisle and bin where I can find it. But I can also ask an associate to check for it on their Zebra/Motorola mobile device. The device also serves as a walkie-talkie, inventory management tool, and even as a mobile point-of-sale unit. Lowes, the competing DIY store, is trying out OSHbots that similarly can guide you to the exact aisle and bin, and even tell you if the item is not in stock so you can save yourself the walk.

As you follow the OSHbot it also displays ads for related items. It is multilingual and also communicates with employees, the inventory information and summarizes items that customers requested but the store does not offer.

Go to the Home Depot paint department with a scrape from your wall or door as tiny as your fingernail, and the MatchRite sensor and Behr software will mix you a can of near-perfectly-matched paint. The hardware department can duplicate a wide variety of keys—and even reproduce some car fobs with electronic chips—using equipment from The Hillman Group. Try the NCR self-checkout register with its scale, camera, and speaker plus the bar-code and credit-card scanner. Check out the AmeriGas vending machine to exchange propane tanks.

Walk around and see even more technology in the store's products: The Blossom smart sprinkler controller uses weather Big Data to customize home irrigation: the Osram smart LEDs turn lighting into an art form: the Nest thermostat learns from your usage patterns, the Canary Doorbell comes with motion sensors and high-def camera: the EGO lawn mower is cordless with a lithium-ion battery; and the Nexgrill Evolution grill has infrared technology.

There may not be a Genius Bar at Home Depot, but associates in the store can provide details on most of these products. Like I said, the average Home Depot employee has evolved quite a bit, surrounded by all this technology.

The Platform Economy

Tony DiBenedetto lives a few miles from us, but the experiment he describes could easily have been done from our street or a growing number of streets around the world. DiBenedetto, CEO of Tribridge, an IT systems integrator, realized he was using his Chevy Volt less than 5% of the time.

> "I started taking Uber, and I start journaling about every single trip. I did it for about 30 days, and I drew a number

of conclusions that led me to sell my car. Firstly, it was very accessible, so the idea there wouldn't be cars, or there'd be these long waits, just isn't true. My average wait time is about four to five minutes. So I did the smart systems thing: I worked backward and said, five minutes before I wanted to leave I would order a ride on the Uber app, and calculate when I should go downstairs or go out of my house. I got the wait time down to one or two minutes. That is one of those myths about, 'Oh, you have to wait a long time.'

The second misconception was that you would get unqualified drivers, and really at the end of the day you get normal, hardworking people.

Third, I noticed that my mood was better. Instead of being stressed out, I'd just let the driver deal with the traffic. By the time I got to work I was relaxed. Maybe I had checked email, maybe I listened to music . . . just a very different ride to work and a very different ride back.

I save a couple of extra hundred bucks a month, but it's less about the money. The stress is a much bigger factor and I didn't even mention the time efficiency. If you drive to downtown Tampa, you have to add ten minutes to find a parking spot. The other side effect is that now that people know I do not have a car, they give me rides all the time. I'm 'that guy' now, I'm the hippie, bumming a ride with my thumb out. It's just funny, you know? It's become a little bit of a movement, because I've got other people saying, 'maybe I should try that.'"

Next, he looked for opportunities across his company:

"I took a look at our company's T&E and our people are renting a ton of cars. So I got my whole exec team to stop renting cars, then I rolled Uber out to the whole company, and we've documented the savings. We're saving 35% on T&E because we're not using rental cars and taxis."

After the hundreds of Uber rides he has taken, I asked him if he had drawn a demographic profile of the drivers:

> "Most of them were not ex-taxi drivers. I would say 50% of the people who drove me in that first month had a second job. It was everything from young kids just trying to make it, to retired people, or people who were bored. One of my drivers was a helicopter pilot who, for two weeks a month, worked for the big oil companies in New Orleans. The other two weeks he just didn't see himself doing nothing. He's ex-military, and so he picked up the Uber thing to basically not be bored. I thought that was interesting. The retired people were all pretty similar: They wanted to get out of the house or make a little extra cash. I'd say 5% to 10% were in between jobs. There's no question that it fills a gap in employment. It allows for people to run their little businesses, and still do Uber as a supplement. All the drivers love the flexibility."

While DiBenedetto is describing Uber (and other on-demand transportation services like Lyft) from his personal perspective, we are seeing a technology platform change the nature of work and the nature of the commute. It is an example of the "gig economy" where workers work for multiple employers, work when they decide to, and where demand patterns influence pricing (like Uber's surge fares). With its UberPool service clocking over 100 million trips since it was launched in August 2014, the company's product variety and popularity continues to grow.

Peter Evans, author of *The Platform Economy*, says Uber as a platform is dwarfed by many others like Amazon and Alibaba. He is VP of the Center for Global Enterprise (CGE), a nonprofit organization which studies the evolution of the contemporary corporation. A CGE survey of over 175 platform companies like Uber showed they have a market value of over $4.3 trillion and employ millions of people, both directly and indirectly. Asia now has the largest number of leading platforms with 82, exceeding those in North America. The ability of platforms to better utilize houses, cars, and workspaces, among other assets, has spawned considerable interest and passion around the potential of the so-called "share economy."[36]

Anshu Sharma talks of the dramatic change such services are bringing to his native India. The former Salesforce.com executive, now an investor, said:

> "The personal chauffeur has the status of domestic help. Some are abused verbally, and may sometimes have to sit long hours in 100-degree weather with air conditioning turned off. The life of a personal chauffeur can be tough and it can also get boring: Listening to the same husband and wife arguments for years can be downright annoying. Uber and Ola [an Indian ride-sharing service] now offer these drivers an unprecedented opportunity—to be free, decide their own hours, and become owner/entrepreneurs. These ride-sharing services often offer generous support to help them get cars and car loans—which can be hugely challenging in India for people with relatively low income or savings. Banks typically only lend to the well-heeled upper classes."

India is dwarfed by China in the adoption of such ride-sharing models. Didi Kuaidi, China's Uber, claims to have handled over a billion rides in 2015 alone. In comparison, it took Uber five years to reach that milestone.

High-Tech Paper

Our region in Florida, with its theme parks, beaches, and other attractions, gets plenty of tourists. Only a few, however, go on

---

[36] http://thecge.net/the-center-for-global-enterprise-releases-first-global-platform-survey-valuing-platform-based-companies-at-4-3-trillion/

tours, courtesy of Valpak and Amazon, that would qualify as *Charlie and the Chocolate Factory* fantasies for most technologists.

The 470,000-square-foot Valpak plant in St. Petersburg produces something truly low-tech—the paper coupons that get you discounts at stores and restaurants. Yet it is highly automated. You have to be extremely mechanized when you print over 50 billion pieces of paper a year and stuff them into 500 million envelopes (the distinctive Valpak blue ones) to be mailed to 40 million unique addresses across the country.

As part of Cox Media Group, the coupon distributor leverages the Big Data that comes from the parent group's 31 million TV viewers, 3.5 million print and online newspaper readers, and 14 million radio listeners.

The plant's printing, packing, and sorting technology comes from 20 different vendor systems, and is integrated through the SAP ERP system. It reduces the previous process of manufacturing down from four days to four hours.

And it had to factor in the challenges found in our paradise. The facility is built to withstand hurricanes and lightning strikes, and to run for up to two weeks "off the grid."

That's a lot of automation around a paper product!

Amazon's recently opened fulfillment centers in Ruskin and Lakeland are each twice as large as the Valpak center. They are designed for speed, driven by the move to same day and Sunday delivery in the grocery/retail business. Within minutes of orders being clicked by customers, Kiva robots start picking the items and bringing them to humans to inspect and pack. The short (a little over a foot), square, yellow robots whiz around and carry pods (tall racks) with items weighing up to 700 pounds. Instead of humans walking around those giant facilities, the items are brought to them, shaving time on each package. The Lakeland facility, which ships larger items than the Ruskin center, also boasts the Robo-Stow, which stacks pallets of merchandise. It's huge—as big as an adult African elephant.

(No tour would be complete without trivia: The first item sold from the Lakeland center was a CreativeWare 2-Tier Buffet Server, and from Ruskin it was an Anna doll from the Disney movie *Frozen*.)

Meanwhile, at Amazon's Davenport distribution center, the whizbang is found in the sorting technology with its miles of conveyor belts. This center receives packages from other locations, sorts them by ZIP code, and stacks them six feet high on pallets before trucking them to nearby post offices. It allows Amazon to control each package much longer and further down the delivery "last mile," which helps it to further optimize the shipping process.

In the last few chapters we have seen a wide range of machines work alongside workers and help make the people safer and savvier. In the next chapter, let's look at some patterns around all this automation. Let's also explore why we have such a dysfunctional labor economy with millions of unfilled jobs on the one hand and massive labor discontent on the other.

CHAPTER 5

May You Live in Interesting Times

~~→

For eight seasons, Mike Rowe, host of TV's *Somebody's Gotta Do It,* highlighted some of the grossest work around, including sewer inspector and shark-suit tester. While many of those tasks are well paid, he could have used the 3D neologism for many of them—dull, dirty, and dangerous. The 3Ds mirror the Japanese 3Ks—kitanai, kiken, kitsui—which roughly translate to hard, dirty, and dangerous, a term the *New York Times* used to describe what is often relegated to migrant, guest workers.[37]

Dirty Jobs—or Delightful?

Physical labor is often romanticized in the West. In Japan, and across Asia, such labor is often looked down upon and ill compensated. Across the world, though, whether termed 3K or 3D, such tasks have often been candidates for automation.

---

[37] http://www.nytimes.com/2009/04/23/business/global/23immigrant.html

Tim Cripsey of MFC NetForm, introduced in Chapter 2, describes how automation has helped with 3D tasks on his shop floor:

"Automation helps around repetitive motions. If there's a human action that is repeated, and we're doing 500,000 pieces a year, that action, repetitive on the operator, can lead to carpal tunnel syndrome. There are times when automation is used to load, unload, and move parts, to lower the wear and tear on the human body. There are times when a robot is used because of the working conditions. Imagine you are loading a part into an oily machine. In high volume manufacture like ours, you've got repeated loading and unloading of a machine. The concern here is not about the carpal tunnel or muscle fatigue. It's about the unpleasantness. With today's automation, there's no need for an operator to have to do this dirty job.

Then you have activities, like deburring, which are dangerous. In the past, and even today in some countries, they may have somebody holding a part against a wire brush wheel and taking the sharp edges off. With automation, we don't have to do that. It's not safe. It's just not a good modern day production situation. Do our operators want to be loading a part into an oily, dirty machine? No. Do they want to be lifting something heavy time and time again? No. Do they want to endanger themselves? No. These are three classic situations where the automation helps the operator. There are other areas where automation helps with consistency. It's very hard for a human to precisely load something time and again. Robots have high accuracy."

We have many examples of 3D tasks being automated in the first four chapters. David Truch of BP talked about robotic crawlers and drones to monitor equipment in risky places. The robotic truck arm at Republic Services has replaced the dirty and dangerous job of dangling at the back and emptying hundreds of stinky, heavy bins of garbage. The process bots at ANZ Bank do many of the routine tasks. The Exari software has taken the tedium out of writing many of the contracts. Accounting firms are automating a variety of compliance tasks around routine inventory and cash counts. UPS telematics are allowing its drivers to maintain an impressive safe driving record. TALON robots are helping keep soldiers from harm's way. The infusion pumps at the medical center at UCSF are helping with patient safety. Encryption and other technologies are protecting journalists and allowing them to do investigative projects like the Panama Papers. Robotic harvesters are doing the picking jobs in many orange orchards and vineyards. The computational chemistry advances at Texas A&M are allowing simulations of many lab tests. The Kiva robots are doing the dull and physically tiring work of picking items for the Amazon warehouse employee. Robotic butlers are freeing up hotel employees to be responsive to more complex guest requests.

Deploying automation is not only for the 3D tasks; it's increasingly about pleasing your constituents. We saw how the Golden State Warriors are using technology to improve player and coach performance to the absolute glee of their fans. Pixar is raising the bar for digital animation and creating a new generation of fans for that genre. We saw how Amazon is automating data centers and passing along savings on a regular basis, to the delight of enterprise customers. Foxconn has blended robots with thousands of jobs for young Chinese workers and delivered billions of high-quality Apple devices. The Hadid technology-enabled architecture draws gasps from visitors around the globe. Robotic surgeries lead to smaller incisions, less blood loss, and higher patient satisfaction.

In many ways, automation is also leading to more sustainable practices. Automated irrigation in wineries is allowing for better water management. The automation of research at Hampton Creek may lead to less use of animal products.

Accenture, in their white paper on Intelligent Automation, points to other examples:

"Many pioneering companies are now deploying intelligent automation to transform their use of data. Paxata is showing data scientists where to focus their efforts by automatically finding meaningful relationships within vast data lakes. Adobe Target has automated not just the personalization of ad experiences, but the creation of experiments on those experiences to figure what features a consumer will find compelling, thereby enabling marketing executives to test their ideas without involving IT. Pointing the way ahead, Bloomsbury.ai, a London-based start-up, has announced plans to release a demo enabling people with no programming skills to carry out complex data analytics. Bloomsbury.ai claims that, with training, its technology could be used for everything from art creation to consumer products. It's not just in IT systems that automation is driving real change. It's happening out in the physical world, too: improving mining safety by letting men and machines work side by side in a way that takes the most dangerous tasks off the shoulders of people (e.g., intelligent 'worms' monitoring hazardous mining operations), changing the rules of e-commerce by driving ever closer to same-day delivery (e.g., 30,000 Kiva robots helping Amazon to meet rising customer demand), easing urbanites' lives with intelligent street lighting and predictive traffic control, and boosting crop yields through precision agriculture (e.g., companies such as AquaSpy and AGCO, which are already using intelligent automation to support 'digital' farming)."[38]

---

[38] https://www.accenture.com/t20160125T111718__w__/us-en/_acnmedia/Accenture/Omobono/TechnologyVision/pdf/Intelligent-Automation-Technology-Vision-2016.pdf#zoom=50

As machines do more routine work, employees are moving to what demographer Richard Florida calls the "creative class." In a 2014 interview, he talked about changes he had noticed in the prior decade:

> "The thing that's surprised me the most is how thoroughgoing the shift from the old industrial to the new creativity-driven economy has been. In the decade since I delivered *The Rise of the Creative Class* to its publisher, a whole series of events have occurred, from the collapse of the tech bubble and the attacks of 9/11 to the economic and financial meltdown of 2008, any one of which might have been sufficient to derail or reverse the trends the book described. Instead, they have only become more deeply ensconced."[39]

Malcolm Frank, EVP of Strategy at the IT outsourcing firm Cognizant, told me in an interview:

> "We think automation is a big deal. If you look at it from a client perspective, this may be the largest opportunity in a generation to rethink their businesses and find cost savings within their operations."

The strategy consulting firm, McKinsey,[40] has a useful framework in Figure 5-1 where they analyzed 2,000 activities across 800 occupations, and measured each against 18 different capabilities that potentially could be automated.

---

[39] http://www.forbes.com/sites/danschawbel/2014/02/19/richard-florida-economic-trends-all-entrepreneurs-should-follow/#696ee8f9bbe1

[40] http://www.mckinsey.com/business-functions/business-technology/our-insights/four-fundamentals-of-workplace-automation

To grasp the impact of technological automation, we structured our analysis around 2,000 distinct work activities.

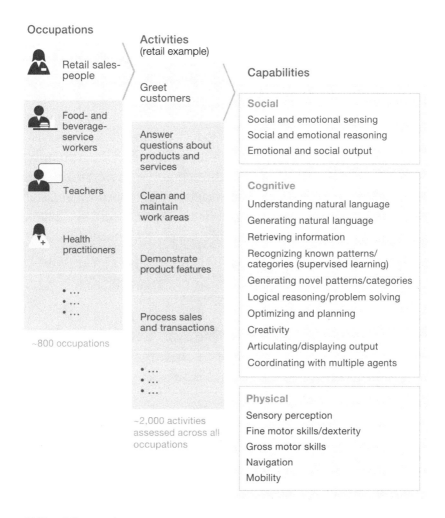

McKinsey&Company | Source: Expert interviews; McKinsey analysis

Figure 5-1   Credit–McKinsey & Co.

McKinsey could have gone further and matched these activities and capabilities to available technologies. In this book, we have already seen how applications of machine learning, robotics, 3-D printing, drones, exoskeletons, and other technologies are changing the nature of work in many industries.

Man-Made Problems

But all is not "blue sky" when it comes to automation technologies. In the next part of the book we will explore both the pessimism that's overtaken much of the world and some strong reasons for a more nuanced, even optimistic perspective. The sky, I firmly believe, is not falling. But, before that exploration, I want to mention some of the primarily man-made problems we face that impinge on our collective ability to make best use of our workers and our machines. In Chapter 11, we will look at related issues and their policy implications in greater depth.

While machines are doing their best to help improve our livelihoods, humans continue to complicate things. Rowe, introduced above, spoke in an interview[41] about five of the damaging job myths we're taught today:

- There are no good jobs left in America.
- The best path to a good job is a four-year degree.
- Trade jobs are dead-end jobs.
- You can't make six figures.
- There's no room for women in the trades.

Frank, introduced above, was at the WEF event at Davos, Switzerland, in early 2016 and he relayed to me that U.S. politics came up early and often in most conversations. He described a German executive who observed, "Half of your voters are angry, on the left with Sanders or the right with Trump. Yet America right now is economically the envy of the world. If the country that's doing the best is that upset, then what does that mean for the rest of us?" Frank said, "I thought that was a very thoughtful perspective."

---

[41] http://www.forbes.com/sites/kathycaprino/2016/05/02/the-dirtiest-man-on-tv-dispels-5-damaging-myths-about-blue-collar-labor/#294e96a97db6

All's Not Well by the Bay

In Chapter 1, we saw young professions in food technology and ancient occupations like winemaking being reshaped by automation. Human-designed policies are also leading to major problems in the Bay Area.

Berkeley has a special place in American history. It has attracted many a young person to move west. In a commencement speech at USC introduced in Chapter 1, Ellison described his own personal journey:

> "I was twenty-one years old when I dropped out of college, packed everything I owned, jeans, t-shirts, leather jacket, guitar, into my car and drove from Chicago to Berkeley, California. Berkeley in the 1960s was at the center of everything. The anti-war movement, the free speech movement, the human rights movement. It was the perfect place for an undisciplined, selfish, twenty-something to begin his search for himself, a righteous cause and a job that he loved. Everyone living in Berkeley in the 1960s opposed the Vietnam War. I was no different. It was the Age of Aquarius but I never had long hair and I never wore love beads. I learned to play popular protest songs on my guitar, but I was never a committed, serious, anti-war protester. I did find a cause, however. One I still feel passionately about today. A few hours east of Berkeley are the Sierra Nevada Mountains. I fell in love with those mountains and the ineffable, natural beauty of Yosemite Valley. I cared about the wilderness and I wanted to help preserve it. I joined the Sierra Club. I became an environmentalist."[42]

People's Park in Berkeley is an icon of the Flower Children vs. Establishment theme that dominated the turbulent '60s. In May 1969, thousands of students rioted there, fighting against

---

[42] https://www.youtube.com/watch?v=5DJaWWwITRM

the police. The site, today a free public park, is sanctuary to the city's large homeless population—and an eyesore. Professor Sam Davis explained his disillusionment:

> "I was present at the inception of People's Park in the spring of 1969. For many years I have also tried through architectural consultation, service on the People's Park Community Advisory Board, and several other park-related committees, to motivate the campus to come to terms with the many problems caused by its neglect. Nothing has happened."[43]

People's Park pales in comparison to the homeless crisis in San Francisco, which no one seems to want to solve. Some journalists have banded together to push for some action:

> "Next month, media organizations in the Bay Area are planning to put aside their rivalries and competitive instincts for a day of coordinated coverage on the homeless crisis in the city. The *Chronicle*, which is leading the effort, is dispensing with traditional news article formats and will put forward possible solutions to the seemingly intractable plight of around 6,000 people without shelter."[44]

Politicians have seen that as an opportunity for more taxes. There is a proposal for what is being called a "tech tax"—the city's tech firms like Twitter would be required to pay a 1.5% payroll tax.

The focus on tech companies reflects a growing resentment. The *New York Times* wrote:

> "Behind the proposal is more than just an effort to raise revenue. The tech tax, the passage of which is considered

---

[43] http://blogs.berkeley.edu/2015/09/29/peoples-park-its-time-for-change/
[44] http://www.nytimes.com/2016/05/16/us/san-francisco-homelessness.html

a long shot, is the latest manifestation of resentment here against the proliferation of high-paid tech workers and the pressures that rising prices have put on residents. Tensions have flared over the notion that tech workers live in a parallel society, in which they are whisked in private buses to work, socialize in their own circles and do not participate in San Francisco's traditions of social collaboration."[45]

That is just the tip of the iceberg. Below the visible homeless, there is a major real estate crisis that is making the Bay Area unattractive to workers. According to an analysis by Zillow, the real estate site:

"A single, entry-level software engineer in Silicon Valley with no additional income beyond their salary can expect to spend more than over half of their after-tax income on housing costs—either to rent or buy—for the median home in the communities where their colleagues typically live. In the Seattle area, the share of income necessary to rent or buy the typical home where local Google/Microsoft workers live hovers around 30 percent, a prudent standard by historic norms."[46]

We are talking about a peninsula with a finite amount of real estate. Yet, in such a market, you would think there would be all kinds of apps and brokerage sites to help with rentals and sublets. Instead, it is a chaotic market where people list and look for places on Craigslist, Airbnb, Homestay.com, and many other sites. It is also leading to scams. As a local Bay Area real-estate blog noted: "Alex Bastian, a spokesman for the San Francisco District Attorney's Office, said the scams have grown common in the past few years and tend to come in waves. The crime often

---

[45] http://www.nytimes.com/2016/07/05/us/san-francisco-considers-tax-on-tech-companies-to-pay-for-booms-downside.html?_r=1
[46] http://www.zillow.com/research/living-costs-silicon-valley-seattle-12314/

originates from outside the U.S. but relies on a local middleman who collects the fraudulent payments, he said. Many times the local contact is also a victim of the scam and believes the payment is for an unrelated purpose, Bastian noted."[47]

An even bigger crisis looms due to the Valley's ambivalence related to ethical use of machines. In 1942, science fiction writer Isaac Asimov defined what are even today known as Asimov's Three Laws of Robotics:[48]

- A robot may not injure a human being or, through inaction, allow a human being to come to harm.

- A robot must obey the orders given it by human beings except where such orders would conflict with the First Law.

- A robot must protect its own existence as long as such protection does not conflict with the First or Second Laws.

He later introduced a fourth law:

- A robot may not harm humanity, or, by inaction, allow humanity to come to harm.

Since then, we have developed so much software and smart machines that ethical issues keep proliferating. In my 2010 book, *The New Polymath*, I dedicated a whole chapter titled "Ethics: In an Age of Cyberwar and Cloning." In that, I wrote:

"There has arisen a growing body of cyberethical issues regarding privacy, God powers related to genetics and nanotechnology, the food/biofuel trade-off issues, crime in virtual worlds, and others."[49]

---

[47] http://blog.pacificunion.com/bay-area-rental-scams-rise/
[48] https://en.wikipedia.org/wiki/Three_Laws_of_Robotics
[49] https://www.amazon.com/New-Polymath-Profiles-Compound-Technology-Innovations/dp/0470618302/ref=sr_1_1?s=books&ie=UTF8&qid=1468022781&sr=1-1&keywords=the+new+polymath

and I asked:

> "Go to most hospitals and they can quickly convene an
> ethics committee, which often includes a doctor, nurse,
> social worker, attorney, chaplain, medical ethics profes-
> sional, and a member of the community. The committee
> is available to a doctor or someone close to a patient to
> consult on an ever-evolving set of issues from genetic
> testing to euthanasia.
>
> While individual technology vendors may not have
> enough ethical issues themselves, across the technology
> industry, should it consider establishing similar ethics
> committees?"

Individual tech executives in the Bay Area step up to such
ethical issues from time to time. Bill Joy, cofounder of Sun
Microsystems, in his 2000 article titled "Why the Future Doesn't
Need Us,"[50] raised significant ethical issues regarding nanotechnology, genetics, and robotics.

More recently, Elon Musk, founder of Tesla and SpaceX, Steve
Wozniak, founder of Apple, and others cosigned a letter that
warned:

> "Autonomous weapons select and engage targets without
> human intervention. They might include, for example, armed
> quadcopters that can search for and eliminate people meet-
> ing certain predefined criteria, but do not include cruise
> missiles or remotely piloted drones for which humans make
> all targeting decisions. Artificial Intelligence (AI) technol-
> ogy has reached a point where the deployment of such
> systems is—practically if not legally—feasible within years,
> not decades, and the stakes are high: autonomous weapons

---

[50] www.wired.com/wired/archive/8.04/joy.html

have been described as the third revolution in warfare, after gunpowder and nuclear arms."[51]

Silicon Valley executives have taken more of an activist role recently when it comes to social issues. Marc Benioff, CEO of Salesforce, has been especially prominent. The *Wall Street Journal* wrote about him:

> "The 51-year-old Mr. Benioff earlier this year helped push Georgia's governor into vetoing that state's bill that would have let faith-based organizations decline services or fire employees over religious beliefs after the U.S. Supreme Court ruling that backed same-sex marriage. Last year, he and other CEOs were instrumental in persuading Indiana's governor to revise a similar law. He is now pressing cohorts to back measures to close the gender pay gap."[52]

We will need similar leadership from Silicon Valley on ethical issues related to machines that are increasingly participating in our workplaces. For example, if a child dashes in the path of an autonomous car, should it swerve and potentially end up harming its occupants? Should we, as Hollywood is doing in movies like *Good Kill*, tackle the ethics behind drone warfare? Should we allow navigation apps like Waze which may be turning our neighborhood streets into highways? These are the types of sticky questions we will have to face as automation further defines our jobs and lifestyles. And humans need to address them and not expect answers from machines.

Underutilizing the Most Digitally Savvy Generation
I sat in the back of the room as Oracle CEO Mark Hurd presented at the company's HCM conference in Chicago in March 2016. The

---

[51] http://futureoflife.org/open-letter-autonomous-weapons/
[52] http://www.wsj.com/articles/salesforces-marc-benioff-has-kicked-off-new-era-of-corporate-social-activism-1462201172

audience of HR executives seemed surprised when he shared that 38% of Oracle's employee base are Millennials and that they are hiring thousands of graduates straight out of college every year. The feeling seemed to be—this is not Google; why is a legacy software company hiring so many young folks?

There was even more surprise when Hurd confessed he had originally bought into many "myths" about Millennials—that they feel more entitled, that they are not as loyal to employers, that they care more about flexibility than pay or career. Over time and based on plenty of data (he likes detailed metrics in every aspect of business), Hurd presented that "all generations adopt technology at about the same rate," "all are looking for respect and recognition at work," and "all care about career development."

It's been nearly a decade since John Palfrey and Urs Gasser wrote their book *Born Digital: Understanding the First Generation of Digital Natives*. Many of those young kids, and the generation after them, have grown up with iPads, HDTV, electric cars, solar panels at home, and drones and robots as toys. In many ways, they have the ideal mind-set and skill set for our "Silicon Collar" economy.

Books like *Battle Hymn of the Tiger Mother* by Amy Chua, *Lean In* by Sheryl Sandberg, and *Disrupted* by Dan Lyons—and the intense debates raised by these books—reflect the ethnic, sexist, and ageist complexities most companies have to factor in their workforce decisions. Somewhat lost in those conversations is the fact that the digital natives are not adequately participating in our Silicon Collar economy. Youth unemployment is skyrocketing—even in developed countries like Spain, unemployment in the youth under 25 is at a seasonally adjusted 45%. Even worse, in many parts of the world, some youths—frustrated with their lack of opportunity—are using their digital savvy to cause social unrest and even terrorism.

In the U.S., we have burdened 40 million, mostly young adult workers with over $1.3 trillion in student debt, up more than 80%

since the recession. As anthropologist David Graeber poignantly summarized:

> "Student loans are destroying the imagination of youth. If there's a way of a society committing mass suicide, what better way than to take all the youngest, most energetic, creative, joyous people in your society and saddle them with, like, $50,000 of debt so they have to be slaves?"[53]

I have listened to Dennis Howlett, introduced in Chapter 2, often lament about how the apprenticeship model he grew up with in the UK has disappeared:

> "Older people tend to view the world through dewy eyes, yet there was a time, call it the 'good old days,' when learning a trade or profession had genuine value for everyone. Apprenticeships have a storied history going back centuries. A lad or lass would spend years learning how to lay bricks, bend metal, enter debits and credits correctly, sew back body parts, and on and on. But ever since the advent of robots in manufacturing and the violent swings in the property markets, those opportunities to learn have all but vanished.
>
> We still need houses but today many can be designed and 'built' inside a factory. We still need cars but the machines can be programmed to bend, machine, and mill the parts. We still need balance sheets but machines can (mostly) figure out where to put the associated debits and credits. We haven't quite figured out how to sew back body parts without requiring human skills.
>
> So the burning question comes—who will program the machines? Who will have the creative skills to understand

---

[53] http://www.truthdig.com/avbooth/item/david_graeber_there_has_been_a_war_on_the_human_imagination_20130812http://www.truthdig.com/avbooth/item/david_graeber_there_has_been_a_war_on_the_human_imagination_20130812

the interplay between form and function? Where will the creative minds be nurtured to learn the balance between beauty and aesthetics? At least some of that can be taught and learned; the rest will come down to nurturing the creative mind through mentoring in the old-fashioned apprentice manner. If not, then we are truly lost."

More Man-Made Problems—Affecting Women

In Chapter 3, we saw a number of highly accomplished women and how they are leveraging technology. But for every woman profiled there, it is a major concern that many more are unchallenged and underutilized when it comes to our labor economy.

In the annual letter for the Bill and Melinda Gates Foundation, Melinda Gates in 2016 focused on "unpaid work" in our daily lives and how women disproportionately bear the burden:

"When it comes to Recognize, Reduce, and Redistribute, the story of Anna and Sanare, the couple I stayed with in Tanzania, is pretty inspiring. When they got married, Anna moved from a lush part of the country to live in Sanare's drought-ridden area. She had a hard time adjusting to the extra work that meant. Finally, Sanare came home one day to see Anna sitting on the steps ready to leave, her bags packed and their first child, Robert, in her arms. Sanare, heartbroken, asked how he could persuade her to stay. "Fetch water," she said, "so I can nurse our son." And so, 'Recognizing' the imbalance, Sanare did that. He started walking the miles to the well every day. At first the other village men made fun of him and even accused Anna of witchcraft. But when he said, "My son will be healthier because I'm doing this," they started 'Redistributing' the work with him. After a while, when they got sick of working so hard, they decided to build water tanks to collect rainwater near the village. Now that they've 'Reduced,' no matter who goes to get water, Anna or Sanare, it's a lot closer—and they both spend more time with Robert and their other kids . . ."[54]

She called for innovations to reduce this "time poverty":

> "Can you imagine a machine that washes clothes using no electricity and very little water? Perhaps you can improve on the mortar and pestle, the 40,000-year-old technology I see women using to grind grain into food every time I travel in sub-Saharan Africa or South Asia."

Working as a PwC consultant, I spent several years in the 1980s implementing systems in Saudi Arabia. I do not recall a single conversation with a Saudi woman—in that conservative society, men, particularly foreign expats, are discouraged from engaging in such communication. But I had a number of conversations with Egyptian, Pakistani, and U.S. Muslim women about the state of female workers in the Middle East, and there was an optimism that a significant change was coming. Clearly, 30 years later, that change has not happened, but with Saudi Arabia feeling the pressure to diversify from its dependence on oil, an unintended consequence may be that the role of women in society also changes.

FastCompany wrote about the impact of the ride-sharing service, Uber, on Saudi women:

> "Women in Saudi Arabia are not allowed to drive, leaving them reliant on male relatives or paid services to get to stores, school, and (increasingly) work. So when Uber launched in Riyadh in early 2014, its impact went beyond the general convenience of tech-enhanced ride hailing. The company has made a real difference in Saudi women's mobility."[55]

---

[54] https://www.gatesnotes.com/2016-Annual-Letter
[55] http://www.fastcompany.com/3048461/app-economy/how-uber-is-changing-life-for-women-in-saudi-arabia

The *New York Times* added:

> "Roughly 80 percent of Uber's riders in Saudi Arabia are women, according to the company. Uber has sought to aid the kingdom's Vision 2030 plan, which includes more than doubling the number of women in the overall work force by 2030, to 30 percent."[56]

Uber recently received a significant $3.5 billion investment from the Saudi Public Investment Fund.

The *Times* continued:

> "Princess Reema bin Bandar al-Saud, who sits on Uber's public policy advisory board, has worked with Uber to usher the service into the country, and has the support of female users of the service, said in an interview that the investment was a clear sign of change coming to the region."

Clouds in the Sunshine State

As we have seen in Chapter 4, technology is helping all kinds of workers in the Tampa Bay area and across the rest of Florida, yet there is plenty of economic turmoil.

Florida has always attracted retirees. But *USA Today* described how, with pensions disappearing, aging workers need to stay on jobs much longer:

> "From 1980 through 2015, the proportion of private wage and salary workers participating in defined benefit pension plans fell from 38% to 15%, according to the U.S. Bureau of Labor Statistics. DB plans are the traditional pension plans that your father or grandfather's generation were accustomed

---

[56] http://www.nytimes.com/2016/06/02/technology/uber-investment-saudi-arabia.html

to, but now they're as rare as a gold watch at retirement. The U.S. government later created the 401(k) in 1978, but it was never expected to support workers through retirement. It has been embraced by corporations as a way to attract workers by having the workers pay for their own retirement, thus eliminating pensions from corporate balance sheets. Currently, about 43% of private workers take part in their 401(k) or other defined contribution plan, according to the U.S. BLS. That isn't enough to support most of the retirees throughout their retirement."[57]

Florida, with its mostly service economy, is especially sensitive to minimum wage debates.

Nick Hanauer is not a socialist politician. He is a very successful Seattle-based entrepreneur, yet in an essay in *Politico* he powerfully argued for a higher wage:

"The only way to slash government for real is to go back to basic economic principles: You have to reduce the demand for government. If people are getting $15 an hour or more, they don't need food stamps. They don't need rent assistance. They don't need you and me to pay for their medical care. If the consumer middle class is back, buying and shopping, then it stands to reason you won't need as large a welfare state. And at the same time, revenues from payroll and sales taxes would rise, reducing the deficit. Balancing the power of workers and billionaires by raising the minimum wage isn't bad for capitalism. It's an indispensable tool that smart capitalists use to make capitalism stable and sustainable. And no one has a bigger stake in that than zillionaires like us."[58]

---

[57] http://www.usatoday.com/story/money/2016/04/23/pensions-economy-workers/83292892/
[58] http://www.topinfopost.com/2014/06/30/ultra-rich-mans-letter-to-my-fellow-filthy-rich-americans-the-pitchforks-are-coming

At the other extreme is Ed Rensi, former President and CEO of McDonald's USA, who explained in a *Forbes* column the ripple effect of raising the minimum wage to $15 an hour, a move that he says will drive many franchises to replace jobs with kiosks, as is common in Europe:

> "Over four million people in the U.S. are employed at "limited service" restaurants, a descriptor which includes companies like McDonald's. If even one out of every four jobs was automated, that's one million fewer job opportunities in a country where the youth unemployment rate is more than three times the overall unemployment rate . . . . These young adults who face long spells of unemployment now are at a long-term disadvantage relative to their employed counterparts. One study released by the Employment Policies Institute found that high-school seniors with part-time work experience earned 20% more per year on average, 6–9 years after graduating, relative to their fellow students who didn't work."[59]

Florida also has a heavy mix of migrant labor. The U.S. Department of Housing and Urban Development provides a glimpse at the changing demographic of this labor pool:

> "The face of the farmworker changes from time to time as immigration laws change. Although farmwork is an honorable profession, the annual income is around $7,000 for a single worker and about $10,000 for a family. These numbers encourage workers to leave the fields and move into other vocations. In Florida, many workers remain in the agricultural field, but will find year-round, full-time employment in nurseries. Many others will move into landscaping, construction labor, auto mechanics, etc. To fill the void left when

---

[59] http://www.forbes.com/forbes/welcome/

workers move on, other immigrants move in. Frequently, the first to come is the male head of the household. Currently, at least 50% of the farmworkers in many parts of Florida are here alone. Many of these, though classified as "single," are married men temporarily removed from their families."[60]

In the last few chapters, we have looked at the work of highly worshipped basketball players, masterful architects, and far more modest garbage collectors—all deeply influenced by technology. The executives we interviewed discussed the continuing *human* involvement, and how it is moving jobs to higher level, more creative tasks. However, the fact that so many of these dull, dirty, and dangerous tasks are being automated along with the exponential growth in machine power are leading to widespread panic about jobless futures.

Let's explore this pessimism in detail in the next part of the book.

---

[60] http://portal.hud.gov/hudportal/HUD?src=/states/florida/working/farmworker/commonquestions

Machines as Overlords?

CHAPTER 6

The Sum of All Fears

〜➤

The interviews I conducted for the preceding chapters show practitioners in a wide array of industries using technology to improve productivity and product quality. They were pragmatic and generally optimistic. In the backdrop, as I was conducting these interviews I also found a contrasting sense of pessimism in the academic and analyst world about massive job losses.

Grim Stirrings

Dr. Mark Kamlet, Professor of Economics and Public Policy and Provost Emeritus, has started a research project with Dr. Seth Goldstein, Associate Professor in the Computer Science department at Carnegie Mellon University, a highly respected name in the scientific and engineering world.

He described it to me as follows:

> "We have seen for the last four decades little growth of median wages in the U.S. We are seeing a hollowing out in the center. We are using data from the Bureau of Labor Statistics and other government sources in our research project to develop sophisticated models and simulations of the economy across a wide range of job stratifications to better understand the phenomenon.

We are looking at the impact of technologies on different job categories—obviously paying attention to Big Data and machine learning. But we are also looking at additive and 3-D printing, synthetic biology, and biotech. Our belief is that these technologies are different than those that characterized the agricultural revolution, the first industrial revolution (with inventions like the steam engine), and the second industrial revolution (with inventions like the internal combustion engine). Everybody has always said that the Luddites were wrong—and they *were* wrong. [Luddites were 19th-century English textile workers who sabotaged labor-saving machines the industry was introducing.] They were wrong in the agricultural revolution, and also in the first and second industrial revolutions. At the end of the day, humans did well as a factor of production. It took a lot of time, particularly in the first industrial revolution, but they ended up moving into positions where all the segments of society were earning more.

But the current technology wave is different. Many of today's technologies are increasing their capabilities exponentially, and that was not the case, or certainly not nearly as much, in these earlier technology revolutions."

Dr. Kamlet then invoked Nobel Prize-winning economist Wassily Leontief, who had described how horses had lost out their roles in production chains, and Abraham Maslow, who is well known for his work around human motivation:

"Our basic proposition is that just like horses lost their standing as an important factor of production during the second technology revolution, humans won't be needed quite so much as factors for production moving into the future. They will be like the horse during the second industrial revolution.

If we are correct, this will lead to two existential problems for humans. How are humans going to get the resources to thrive? What will humans do to find fulfillment in settings very different from today where we are defined by our vocations? We are also thinking of ways society might have to be structured—transfer payment programs and the role of the government needed to address what lies ahead.

We have relatively scant experience as a species living in, let alone designing, our economic systems for the higher levels of Maslow's hierarchy. There are deep and interesting computer science problems to be tackled in order to create an economic system based on a computer-mediated system of barter and reputation which will allow people to turn time spent on their avocation into a means of acquiring 'money' to trade for goods and services. Doing so may be one way we can repurpose our lives toward pursuing self-actualization instead of just trying to meet our physiological needs."

Vivek Wadhwa has impressive credentials as a Fellow at the Rock Center for Corporate Governance at Stanford University, Director of Research at the Center for Entrepreneurship and Research Commercialization at Duke, and Distinguished Fellow at Singularity University (an influential Silicon Valley think tank). His past appointments include Harvard Law School, University of California Berkeley, and Emory University. He expressed a view similar to Dr. Kamlet's in a column in the *Washington Post*:

"The technology elite who are leading this revolution will reassure you that there is nothing to worry about because we will create new jobs just as we did in previous centuries when the economy transitioned from agrarian to industrial to knowledge-based. Tech mogul Marc Andreessen has called the notion of a jobless future a 'Luddite fallacy,' referring to past fears that machines would take human jobs away. Those fears turned out to be unfounded because we created newer and better jobs and were much better off.

True, we are living better lives. But what is missing from these arguments is the timeframe over which the transitions occurred. The industrial revolution unfolded over centuries. Today's technology revolutions are happening within years. We will surely create a few intellectually-challenging jobs, but we won't be able to retrain the workers who lose today's jobs. They will experience the same unemployment and despair that their forefathers did. It is they who we need to worry about."[61]

Oxford University in the UK is the oldest university in the English-speaking world. It has observed every revolution mentioned above by Dr. Kamlet and many more. Two of its researchers, Carl Benedikt Frey and Michael A. Osborne, studied 702 occupations using U.S. Bureau of Labor Statistics (BLS) data in their 2013 study titled "The Future of Employment: How susceptible are jobs to computerisation?"

They looked at three sets of "bottlenecks" to computerization: "perception and manipulation tasks" such as finger dexterity; "social intelligence tasks" such as negotiation or persuasion; and "creative intelligence tasks" such as originality.

Their conclusion:

> "According to our estimates, about 47% of total U.S. employment is at risk. We further provide evidence that wages and educational attainment exhibit a strong negative relationship with an occupation's probability of computerisation."[62]

As is common in academia, the Oxford work has been widely quoted by peers around the world, just as they themselves quote

---

[61] https://www.washingtonpost.com/news/innovations/wp/2015/07/07/sorry-but-the-jobless-future-isnt-a-luddite-fallacy/
[62] http://www.futuretech.ox.ac.uk/news-release-oxford-martin-school-study-shows-nearly-half-us-jobs-could-be-risk-computerisation

the work of several MIT professors in their paper. They cite the 2011 book, *Race Against the Machine,* by Erik Brynjolfsson and Andrew McAfee. The book "makes the case that employment prospects are grim for many today not because technology has stagnated, but instead because we humans and our organizations aren't keeping up."[63]

Brynjolfsson and McAfee followed up with their 2014 book, *The Second Machine Age*:

> "Rapid and accelerating digitization is likely to bring eco-nomic rather than environmental disruption, stemming from the fact that as computers get more powerful, companies have less need for some kinds of workers. Technological progress is going to leave behind some people, perhaps even a lot of people, as it races ahead. As we'll demonstrate, there's never been a better time to be a worker with special skills or the right education, because these people can use technology to create and capture value. However, there's never been a worse time to be a worker with only 'ordinary' skills and abilities to offer, because computers, robots, and other digital technologies are acquiring these skills and abilities at an extraordinary rate."[64]

The Oxford professors cite another MIT professor, David Autor, who has long analyzed labor demographics. He coauthored a *New York Times* column which said:

> "Computerization has therefore fostered a polarization of employment, with job growth concentrated in both the highest- and lowest-paid occupations, while jobs in the middle have declined . . . . Demand for highly educated workers who

---

[63] http://www.amazon.com/Race-Against-Machine-Accelerating-Productivity/dp/0984725113/ref=sr_1_4?s=books&ie=UTF8&qid=1460991044&sr=1-4&keywords=andrew+mcafee
[64] http://www.amazon.com/The-Second-Machine-Age-Technologies/dp/0393239357

excel in abstract tasks is robust, but the middle of the labor market, where the routine task-intensive jobs lie, is sagging. Workers without college education therefore concentrate in manual task-intensive jobs—like food services, cleaning and security—which are numerous but offer low wages, precarious job security and few prospects for upward mobility. This bifurcation of job opportunities has contributed to the historic rise in income inequality."[65]

Speaking of societal inequality, the name Thomas Piketty pops up quite often. A Professor (Directeur d'Études) at the École des Hautes Études en Sciences Sociales (EHESS), the Paris School of Economics, and the London School of Economics, he is the author of the best-selling book, *Capital in the Twenty-First Century* (2013),[66] which "emphasizes the themes of his work on wealth concentrations and distribution over the past 250 years. The book argues that the rate of capital return in developed countries is persistently greater than the rate of economic growth, and that this will cause wealth inequality to increase in the future."

The 2016 elections in the U.S. has also brought in politicians like Presidential candidate Bernie Sanders who have amplified the conversation about inequality. U.S. President Barack Obama has tried to explain popular anger in this fashion:

> "Some people are still recovering from the trauma of what happened in 2007–2008. You know, we went through a really scary time. It was the fastest contraction that we've seen even before the Great Depression. By some measures the economy contracted faster and saw a steeper decline than you saw back in the late '20s, early '30s. People still remember the uncertainty that came from their pensions shrinking. Their

---

[65] http://opinionator.blogs.nytimes.com/2013/08/24/how-technology-wrecks-the-middle-class/?_r=0

[66] http://www.amazon.com/Thomas-Piketty/e/B004MZ9VCW/ref=dp_byline_cont_book_1

home values dropping precipitously . . . losing a job. And so I think there's still an insecurity there."[67]

However, even the White House, in its 2016 Economic Report of the President, included automation scores from the Oxford study mentioned above:

> "To better understand the relationship between automation and wages at the occupational level, CEA [the Council of Economic Advisers] matched an occupation's median hourly wage to the occupational automation scores from Frey and Osborne (2013). The median probability of automation was then calculated for three ranges of hourly wage: less than 20 dollars; 20 to 40 dollars; and more than 40 dollars."[68]

Furthermore, even the venerable Bank of England has warned that "up to 15m jobs in Britain are at risk of being lost to an age of robots where increasingly sophisticated machines do work that was previously the preserve of humans."[69]

Widespread Pessimism

Such pessimism is not limited to academia, politics, and government. My former employer, Gartner, the IT research firm, has made similar provocative predictions. As Peter Sondergaard, Head of Research, told the audience at the firm's 2014 Symposium/IT Expo:

> "Gartner predicts one in three jobs will be converted to software, robots and smart machines by 2025 . . . New digital businesses require less labor; machines will make sense of

---

[67] https://finance.yahoo.com/news/obama-articulates-why-americans-are-so-unhappy-185633246.html#

[68] file:///C:/Users/v/Documents/Silicon%20Collar/White%20House%20Robots.pdf

[69] https://www.theguardian.com/business/2015/nov/12/robots-threaten-low-paid-jobs-says-bank-of-england-chief-economist

data faster than humans can. By 2018, digital business will require 50% fewer business process workers."[70]

McKinsey, in the study introduced in Chapter 5, had a more pragmatic position:

> "Our results to date suggest, first and foremost, that a focus on occupations is misleading. Very few occupations will be automated in their entirety in the near or medium term. Rather, certain activities are more likely to be automated, requiring entire business processes to be transformed, and jobs performed by people to be redefined, much like the bank teller's job was redefined with the advent of ATMs."

However, they quantified a fearful outcome from technologies available today:

> "The bottom line is that 45 percent of work activities could be automated using already demonstrated technology. If the technologies that process and "understand" natural language were to reach the median level of human performance, an additional 13 percent of work activities in the US economy could be automated . . ."[71]

Pew Research polled 1,896 experts in 2014 on the following question: Will networked, automated, artificial intelligence (AI) applications, and robotic devices have displaced more jobs than they have created by 2025? The response:

> "Half of these experts (48%) envision a future in which robots and digital agents have displaced significant numbers of both blue- and white-collar workers—with many

[70] http://www.gartnereventsondemand.com/
[71] http://www.mckinsey.com/business-functions/business-technology/our-insights/four-fundamentals-of-workplace-automation

expressing concern that this will lead to vast increases in income inequality, masses of people who are effectively unemployable, and breakdowns in the social order. The other half of the experts who responded to this survey (52%) expect that technology will not displace more jobs than it creates by 2025. To be sure, this group anticipates that many jobs currently performed by humans will be substantially taken over by robots or digital agents by 2025. But they have faith that human ingenuity will create new jobs, industries, and ways to make a living, just as it has been doing since the dawn of the Industrial Revolution."[72]

At Davos in early 2016, as discussed in Chapter 2, the WEF issued a report which read:

"The Fourth Industrial Revolution, combined with other socio-economic and demographic changes, will transform labour markets in the next five years, leading to a net loss of over 5 million jobs in 15 major developed and emerging economies."[73]

A finding from an Infosys report also issued at Davos showed that the pessimism is creeping into younger workers they polled across nine major economies, split between developed nations in Europe and North America and emerging economic powers in Africa, South America, and Asia:

"Despite the conceptual nature of many of the future challenges facing young people—the growth of automation in the workplace for example—they demonstrate high awareness of the core disruptive forces that are likely to impact their career over the decades ahead. Across all markets, an

---

[72] http://www.pewinternet.org/2014/08/06/future-of-jobs/
[73] https://www.weforum.org/press/2016/01/five-million-jobs-by-2020-the-real-challenge-of-the-fourth-industrial-revolution/

average of four in 10 young people can envision their current job being replaced by a robot or Artificial Intelligence machine over the next decade."[74]

Magazines and newspapers reflect the doom and gloom. Google the words "A world without work" and you find articles in *The Atlantic*, the *New York Times,* and the *Washington Post.* Google "When machines take over" and you find a cover issue of *The New Scientist*, and stories at *BBC News* and *The Telegraph* among others.

"Yup, Things Will Suck"

Beyond the realms of academia, government, and consulting, several other authors have contributed to the conversation.

Martin Ford, based in Silicon Valley, talked about jobless futures in his book, *Rise of the Robots:*

> "A computer winning Jeopardy might seem like a trivial, if impressive, feat, but the same technology is making paralegals redundant as it undertakes electronic discovery, and is soon to do the same for radiologists. And that, no doubt, will only be the beginning."[75]

In the UK, Richard Susskind and Daniel Susskind wrote in their book, *The Future of Professions:*

> "In an Internet society, we will neither need nor want doctors, teachers, accountants, architects, the clergy, consultants, lawyers, and many others, to work as they did in the 20th century."[76]

---

[74] http://images.experienceinfosys.com/Web/Infosys/%7B6139fde3-3fa4-42aa-83db-ca38e78b51e6%7D_Infosys-Amplifying-Human-Potential.pdf
[75] http://www.amazon.com/Rise-Robots-Technology-Threat-Jobless/dp/1480574775
[76] http://www.amazon.com/Future-Professions-Technology-Transform-Experts-ebook/dp/B010N9QJ5M/ref=mt_kindle?_encoding=UTF8&me=

A friend of mine heard a pessimistic presentation at a conference and remarked:

> "There must be some West Coast meme going around about automation and robots. We had a keynote from an author and the upshot was pretty much: yup, that'll suck. The audience, including the MC of the event, was all like 'uh . . . now I'm sad.' It was a weird thing to have as the 'get a recent author in to come and inspire you about whatever this conference cares about' slot."

Jon Collins wrote a pragmatic post titled "10 reasons why nobody is going to be out of a job in the digital world". A reader took the time to post a pessimistic rebuttal three times as long! The response ended with an emphatic "It is only a matter of time before all jobs performed by Human Beings are replaced by AI\robots. It is very naïve to think that it will not happen. It is not a matter of if it will happen it is more a matter of when it will happen."[77]

Talking about raining on parades, LinkedIn CEO Jeff Weiner included the following in a letter to his employees announcing the massive $26 billion Microsoft acquisition offer for his company:

> "Remember that dystopian view of the future in which technology displaces millions of people from their jobs? It's happening. In the last three weeks alone, Foxconn announced it will replace 60,000 factory workers with robots, a former CEO of McDonald's said given rising wages, the same would happen throughout their franchises, Walmart announced plans to start testing drones in its warehouses, and Elon Musk predicted fully autonomous car technology would arrive within two years."[78]

---

[77] https://gigaom.com/2016/03/23/10-reasons-why-nobody-is-going-to-be-out-of-a-job-in-the-digital-world/

[78] https://www.linkedin.com/pulse/linkedin-microsoft-changing-way-world-works-jeff-weiner

Why is a CEO whose company thrives on recruitment of human employees painting such a negative future about jobs? Does LinkedIn think it can provide a safe harbor from all the wreckage it believes is headed our way?

History Repeats Itself?

Such pessimism about jobs tends to be cyclical. An article in *The Atlantic* pointed to historical precedents:

> "This fear is not new. The hope that machines might free us from toil has always been intertwined with the fear that they will rob us of our agency. In the midst of the Great Depression, the economist John Maynard Keynes forecast that technological progress might allow a 15-hour work-week, and abundant leisure, by 2030. But around the same time, President Herbert Hoover received a letter warning that industrial technology was a 'Frankenstein monster' that threatened to upend manufacturing, 'devouring our civilization.' (The letter came from the mayor of Palo Alto, of all places.) In 1962, President John F. Kennedy said, 'If men have the talent to invent new machines that put men out of work, they have the talent to put those men back to work.' But two years later, a committee of scientists and social activists sent an open letter to President Lyndon B. Johnson arguing that 'the cybernation revolution' would create 'a separate nation of the poor, the unskilled, the jobless,' who would be unable either to find work or to afford life's necessities."[79]

Fortunately, not every researcher has arrived at such dire conclusions. Having analyzed 120 years of unemployment trends

---

[79] http://www.theatlantic.com/magazine/archive/2015/07/world-without-work/395294/

since the 1890s, Mark Mills, CEO of Digital Power Group, a tech and investment advisory firm, wrote in *Forbes*:

> "There have been three major spikes in unemployment, all caused by financiers, not by engineers: the railroad and bank failures of the Panic of 1893, the bank failures of the Great Depression, and finally the Great Recession of our era, also stemming from bank failures. And each time, once the bankers and policymakers got their houses in order, businesses, engineers, and entrepreneurs restored growth and employment."[80]

Along similar lines, technology analyst and author Denis Pombriant explained to me in an interview:

> "About every 50 years, almost like clockwork, we have the collective experience that the sky is falling. Nothing could be further from the truth. The last time we saw a combination of stagnant wages, poor job growth and even inflation, in the 1970s, we were all sure the world was coming to an end and we blamed the Japanese for stealing our manufacturing jobs. That was when color TV manufacturing went to Japan because they had invested in better glassblowing to make really large picture tubes. We didn't invest because we couldn't figure out how to make money at it. That was pure commoditization.
>
> But the sky stayed in place. Picture tubes were replaced by LCDs and plasma, and we educated ourselves to be great at programming computers and leveraging the internet. And we invented a few things like social media and handheld computing devices. As that process took

---

[80] http://www.forbes.com/sites/markpmills/2014/08/25/in-the-future-will-only-robots-celebrate-labor-day/#734a672b7eb0

hold, no one woke up in the morning thinking of making a better picture tube. We woke up thinking about venture capital and start-ups.

This periodic upheaval has a name: It's a *Kondratiev cycle* or long economic wave, and these things have been happening at regular, if accelerating, intervals since the Industrial Revolution. We're even getting used to them if you consider how much talk there is about the 'next' industrial revolution.

You can think of a K-wave as having an upside and a downside like any other wave. On the ascent, new industries form, employing many, many people; prices rise, inflation spurts ahead, and we think of these as good times. The downside of the wave is all about consolidating the gains of the rise. So it's full of process improvements, efficiency, and effectiveness. The original innovations that made up the rise become embedded in the economy and commoditized, creating the largest possible markets at the lowest prices.

Consider IT generally and hardware particularly. The smart devices we carry in our pockets have the power that once filled a computer room. We marvel at our ingenuity to make those devices even as we ignore the fact that the old computer room cost millions of dollars and employed many highly educated and skilled people. In contrast, most of us don't know what our devices cost today because it's all embedded in a monthly service fee.

That's just one example. The wheel is turning, and we're at the point of needing to spawn a new, long economic wave. This will happen, too, because you can already see the outlines in the economic distance. The wave will be about converting the economy to one that's based purely on electricity generated through alternatives. It will require a big investment in new infrastructure for power generation, a transport grid, and new modes of consumption. It is happening right now if you know where to look."

Nothing to Fear but Fear Itself?

Few people appeared to have noticed that Gartner's Sondergaard had continued his keynote above with this challenge:

> "Who will build the new platform beyond the nexus and the Internet of Things? Not the robots, at least not yet anyway, so this is not all bad news. It brings us back to talent and your organizational strategy. The new digital start-ups in your business units are thirsting for data analysts, software developers, and cloud vendor management staff, often hiring them faster than you are. They may be experimenting with smart machines, seeking technology expertise you probably don't have."

Many people just picked up on Sondergaard's "one in three jobs will be converted" statement. The fact is that Gartner issues hundreds of similar predictions each year and rarely audits them for future accuracy. It usually assigns a probability to them, as an indicator of its confidence in such a prediction, and the Sondergaard statements did not indicate any such hedge.

While Gartner had a timeline for its projection, the Oxford professors did not even attempt one. Additionally, nobody appears to have mapped the Oxford report to actual employment trends in the job categories they analyzed. The professors had calculated a high 0.79 "susceptibility to computerisation factor" (with 1.0 being the highest) to heavy truck and tractor-trailer drivers. This, when the U.S. trucking industry says driver shortages could reach as high as 175,000 positions by 2024 (even if the industry adopts autonomous trucks, regulations will likely require a driver as a backup). The professors had assigned an even higher factor of 0.84 to cartographers and photogrammetrists (who deduce measurements from images), which the BLS projects as one of the fastest growing occupations over the next decade.[81] They had assigned

---

[81] http://www.bls.gov/ooh/fastest-growing.htm

a yet higher 0.94 factor to accountants and auditors, whereas hiring at U.S. public accounting firms jumped to reach record levels in 2013–2014.

In contrast, they calculated a relatively low 0.35 probability to lawyers just as the profession is reporting an oversupply of talent. As an *American Lawyer* article summarized:

> "Even if the number of law school graduates falls below 35,000 in the coming years, as it likely will, the federal government still predicts that the legal profession will offer too few jobs to absorb them—and an astonishingly high turnover rate for those who do find jobs."[82]

Similarly, few appear to have asked the Oxford professors whether it is all doom and gloom. What about new jobs from the automation and new digital businesses? J.P. Gownder, an analyst at the research firm Forrester, is one of the few to have analyzed the Oxford work, and he estimated that "new automation will cause a net loss of only 9.1 million U.S. jobs by 2025." His numbers are well under the roughly 70 million jobs that Frey and Osbourne believe to be in danger of vaporization.[83]

But like Dr. Kamlet previously noted, many believe deeper pessimism is warranted this time. Why? They use Dr. Wadhwa's argument: "Today's technology revolutions are happening within years."

It is clear that, while automation has been gradually trending up in many job categories, other factors are more impactful on job growth or loss. The reality, however, is that when Oxford, MIT, McKinsey, and Gartner talk, the person on the street and even business executives typically just read the headlines, and when all of these big brands agree on something, it solidifies readers' overall impression—in this case, pessimism.

---

[82] http://www.americanlawyer.com/id=1202748112958/The-Governments-Dismal-Job-Outlook-for-Lawyers#ixzz46fepbBmT
[83] http://www.wired.com/2015/08/robots-will-steal-jobs-theyll-give-us-new-ones/

It is as Winston Churchill once said:

> "Why, you may take the most gallant sailor, the most intrepid airman or the most audacious soldier, put them at a table together—what do you get? The sum of their fears."

The pervasive fear is even leading to discussions about "Universal Basic Income" to prepare for a jobless future (as we will examine in greater depth in Chapter 11). Switzerland held a referendum in June 2016 which would have approved the government paying $2,600 a month to each adult, regardless of work status. While the referendum failed to be approved, a poll done by DemoSCOPE in January 2016 showed 59% of Swiss people under 35 believed basic income will eventually become reality. Young people seem to overwhelmingly support a universal basic income—making it a political likelihood in the decades to come.[84] Similar discussions are happening in Finland, the Netherlands, and several other countries. What is striking is they are assuming automation will kill lots of jobs long before we are sure of that possibility.

All the above does make me wonder, why are so many smart folks so pessimistic?

Pombriant has one explanation:

> "The people crying loudest that the sky is falling can be separated into two buckets. The first bucket contains all those who have never experienced a wave change, which is to say all of us. We've lived our productive lives in one paradigm and we need to figure out what to do when we no longer make metaphorical picture tubes. The second group is all those people who have invested trillions of

---

[84] http://qz.com/699739/why-switzerlands-universal-basic-income-referendum-matters-even-though-failed/

dollars in the current paradigm. All the investment in fossil fuels, for instance, has a shortening half-life and it has to be written off. But the sky isn't falling; we're just experiencing a paradigm shift."

Some would suspect a liberal agenda for more government and welfare programs. But the viewpoints above come from a wide range of academics, analysts, economists, and strategy consultants so I doubt there is a singular political motivation.

My own guess is that the academics and economists are projecting raw computing curves and assuming a linear impact on job curves. In a 1965 paper, Gordon Moore had predicted computing power would double every two years (which is known as Moore's Law). Fifty years hence, has panic finally set in on its impact on jobs? Are people still jittery from the Great Recession of 2008?

But we also know that agriculture used to account for 40% of U.S. employment in 1900, and now accounts for less than 5%. That shift took place over a century, and in many parts of the world the agrarian society is still dominant.

It's About the People, Folks

My own opinion on the question is clearly more optimistic than most of the prognosticators cited before. Perhaps I am watching too much cable TV with its wide range of workers and entrepreneurs in shows like *Cake Boss, Fast N' Loud, Hell's Kitchen, Inside Man, Shark Tank, Top Gear* and *Undercover Boss*—all of which indicate a rapidly changing labor economy.

Or perhaps it's an outcome of writing my books. I research quite a bit, but I also interview between 50 and 100 people for each book. I seek out interviews with experts, artisans, and exemplary executives. And in publishing those books, I am surrounded by many small business people in my publishing and consulting circles who are nowhere near so pessimistic. My first two books were published by John Wiley, a major New York house. In various stages of the books' design, editing, printing, and marketing processes, I figure at least 15 of Wiley's employees or contractors were involved. For the last few books, I have been working with Amazon and thus have been the "project manager"—and have worked with a wide range of designers, graphic artists, editors, printers, and shipping agents. I have "decomposed" the publishing supply chain and found it much more efficient and responsive.

Or possibly, I am hanging around executives in the aerospace industry who talk about explosive capacity growth in their businesses. The sky appears to be no limit for the industry as commercial aviation spreads globally, and as next-gen autonomous and space vehicles take off with a wide range of new applications. And what about those in the U.S. auto industry which had its best sales year ever in 2015? These executives may grumble about trade unions but you can quickly turn the talk to talent they admire and their masterpieces—Bugattis, Mustangs, and Blackbirds.

> Nonetheless, the overall pessimism did make me go back and study the impact of automation on several sectors. What I found and describe in the next chapter is "evolution over decades, not revolution."

CHAPTER 7

Evolution, Not Revolution

⤳

The widespread pessimism described in the previous chapter made me go back and study the impact of automation in several occupations: grocery and retail checkout, public accounting, commercial driving, and the U.S. Postal Service. I wanted to analyze a representative cross-section, so for a good blend I chose something retail, something professional, something "trade," and something governmental.

UPC Codes—Circa 1952

The *New York Times* reported in 1992 on the visit by U.S. President George H.W. Bush to a National Grocers Association convention in Orlando, FL. He had "emerged from 11 years in Washington's choicest executive mansions to confront the modern supermarket."[85] As the article described, "He grabbed a quart of milk, a light bulb and a bag of candy and ran them over an electronic scanner. The look of wonder flickered across his face again as he saw the item and price registered on the cash register screen. 'This is for checking out?' asked Mr. Bush."

His advisers had to come up with excuses why Bush seemed so out of touch with scanners that had become increasingly common in stores since the mid-'70s. Indeed, the Secret Service does,

---

[85] http://www.nytimes.com/1992/02/05/us/bush-encounters-the-supermarket-amazed.html

in fact, prevent the President and Vice President (which Bush had been for eight years under President Ronald Reagan) from doing many things that most regular folks do on a daily basis.

Instead, the advisers could have pointed out that the scanner and the UPC code had been evolving for a long time. The promise of scanners had long been unfulfilled in the grocery business. In fact, it took several fortuitous turns for the technology to be born.

In 1948, Bernard Silver, a Drexel Institute student, overheard a supermarket executive asking the dean of the engineering school for help in automating the checkout process in the midst of the postwar boom in grocery commerce. The dean demurred, but Silver mentioned the conversation to his friend, N. Joseph Woodland. Woodland figured he could use Morse code concepts he had learned as a Boy Scout. While working on the problem at his grandparents' Miami home, there was another lucky turn. Running his hands through the sand at a local beach, Woodland hit on the idea of a bull's-eye made up of a series of concentric circles with an associated scanner. They received a patent for that idea in 1952.

Then their luck seemed to run out. Woodland had joined IBM in 1951, but could not interest them in commercializing the technology. Woodland and Silver eventually sold the patent to Philco in 1962, for $15,000. Considering how ubiquitous UPC codes are today, that was a pittance. RCA (then an IBM competitor) acquired Philco, and in 1967 had limited success with the bull's-eye code at the Kroger grocery store chain. The patent expired in 1969. Two decades after Silver and Woodland had started work on it, the scanner was still mostly a curiosity.

IBM got serious about the opportunity when RCA interested the National Association of Food Chains in 1969 into looking at the idea, and the industry formed a committee on a Uniform Grocery Product Code. Woodland was luckier this time. He worked with other IBM-ers like George Laurer to redesign the UPC, moving to a rectangular row of bars each representing multiple copies of data. It was significantly smaller than the original bull's-eye which was eating up too much "surface area" on the packaging. The bull's-eye also had a smearing problem, making some codes unreadable. This was less of a problem with vertical lines. Other IBM employees at the Rochester, MN laboratory worked on the optics and lasers. IBM became one of the earliest vendors to go to market with a system, called the 3660 (the 3663 terminal and the 3666 scanner). The grocery industry started to encourage food manufacturers and other industries to package their goods with Laurer's version of the UPC code.

Woodland's (and IBM's) luck turned again. On June 26, 1974, a cashier at a Marsh Supermarket in Troy, OH scanned a 10-pack of Wrigley's Juicy Fruit gum. However, it was not on an IBM machine. This UPC code was scanned using a machine made by rival NCR, known then as National Cash Register. The store using an IBM machine came online a week later. NCR would go on to be a leading provider of point-of-sales systems in the retail sector. (The Smithsonian National Museum of American History now holds one of those first scanners.)

The scanner did not, however, kill grocery and retail checkout jobs even as the technology spread from around 100 stores in 1976 to over 2,000 in 1980. The cost and time of checking out customers went down, the accuracy went up, and in-store inventory management systems dramatically improved. Campbell Soup, Kellogg, and many other companies started introducing more varieties of their products. Customer choice grew, and, as a result, retail sales grew. By the early 2000s, bar code technologies had become a $17 billion business, scanning billions of items each day.[86]

In the meantime, UPC and derivative codes spread to other industries. For example, they are indispensable for logistics and tracking of UPS and FedEx packages. They are also found on assembly lines, on passports, and in hospitals where they help match patient and drug data in automatic infusion pumps (as Dr.

---

[86] http://www.slate.com/blogs/the_eye/2014/04/03/a_short_history_of_the_modern_barcode_99_percent_invisible_by_roman_mars.html

Blum had described in Chapter 1). Today, QR codes—a close cousin of UPCs—carry information both vertically and horizontally in a much smaller space than previous-generation bar codes. They help us board planes, teach us features in cars, and have become a marketer's dream: You find them in magazines, at markets, and on restaurant menus.

Six decades after it was patented, even with today's self-checkout kiosks in many stores, the technology has still not killed "retail salespersons," a job the Oxford professors (discussed in the previous chapter) have calculated at a 0.92 factor of susceptibility to automation.

The Accounting Scenario

Let's next turn to "accountants and auditors," a job category to which the Oxford study assigned an even higher susceptibility factor of 0.94.

According to the AICPA report, 2015 Trends in the Supply of Accounting Graduates and the Demand for Public Accounting Recruits, hiring at public accounting firms jumped to record levels in 2013–14. Out of these firms, a whopping 91% said they expected to hire accounting graduates at the same or higher levels in 2015.[87]

What gives? Why are these firms not quaking in their boots about automation and instead are continuing to hire young accountants?

Part of the answer came in Chapter 3 where we pointed out that even though accounting is about numbers, audits tend to involve scores of judgment calls related to internal controls, reviews of contracts, accuracy of statements, and other risk assessments. Auditing firms are starting to use cognitive computing to automate some of these judgment calls, but it is far more complex than automating the abacus.

---

[87] http://www.journalofaccountancy.com/issues/2015/oct/cpa-jobs-public-accounting.html#sthash.YkqZoCoW.dpuf

To obtain a fleshed-out answer to this conundrum, I turned to two professionals; one who has been helping accountants automate many of their functions and another who has spent a lifetime around accountants and understands their psyches.

Patrick Taylor is the CEO of Oversight, which sells solutions designed to assist travel, purchasing card, and accounts payable managers in uncovering possible misuse, fraud, and compliance violations. He says they analyze nearly $2 trillion in expenditures annually at Fortune Global 5000 companies and government agencies.

Taylor shared several examples of automation at his clients. One was able to consolidate the number of people involved in the global expense review process from over 20 people in regional offices to five people in a centralized location. In addition, the client went from reviewing a sample of expense reports manually to an automated review of 100% of transactions for policy violations and behavioral patterns. In the first year alone, the client's compliance factor increased from 70% to 90%, and it has recovered millions of dollars of unapplied credits.

Taylor told me, "A lot of attention is focused on when a credit card is stolen, duplicated, or used by the wrong person. Our automation focuses on the instance where the right person is using their credit card, but are they doing the wrong thing. It's authorized users doing something inappropriate."

His clients can move from sample-based reviews to 100% automated review with an emphasis on policy effectiveness, employee behaviors, and root causes of policy violations. This enables them to lower their card administration overhead and safely increase card-spending limits. That often leads to increased card spend and greater rebates from the card provider and preferred supplier network.

Taylor foresees more regulations "like the Foreign Corrupt Practices Act and the Sunshine Act, where you need to be monitoring the behavior of your field representatives, your sales guys—but really it's everyone—and how they are spending money."

He continued:

> "The Foreign Corrupt Practices Act is focused on politically
> exposed persons, and the Sunshine Act focuses on medical
> professionals, but the two are highly analogous. You can look
> beyond this to warranty fraud, or fraud around any kind of
> customer loyalty programs, where people figure out how to
> game those systems. Many of the patterns you're looking
> for would be the same no matter whether you're talking
> about an airline frequent flier program or frequent shopper
> programs. Other areas we look to expand are in health-care
> billing, and we can look at it from both the providers' and
> payers' sides. Am I accurately billing for what I'm doing, and
> am I paying what should be paid? You have the interesting
> pattern of a fair number of transactions, and the analysis is
> pretty much the same across a wide swath of customers."

Taylor sees his tools commoditizing payment recovery auditors—firms like PRGX that work on a contingent basis and share in
savings. Companies can themselves leverage automation analysis
to prevent a lot of problems:

> "Our point would be that you could beat them to the punch,
> and nip the problems in the bud. Instead of recovering that
> erroneous payment, why make it in the first place? That
> actually is pretty compelling, and with automation you can
> afford to do that."

Could public accounting firms be automating more? He replied:

> "We have spent a lot of years trying to work with them
> because they'd be a natural channel for what we do. It's
> interesting that at the higher-level leadership they see the
> need to automate; they know their continuous recruiting is
> expensive, they grind all these young people out, and there

are real challenges to the long-term, sustainable business model. But while they're global organizations, they are also a combination of microbusinesses. The guy who runs the office in Atlanta has a lot of autonomy. As you get further from the senior leadership, things become more tactical. The business model is to hire a bunch of lower-priced recent college graduates and keep them busy. That's how the manager rises through the ranks. It is predicated on building up that pyramid. What happens out in the field is somewhat disconnected from the leadership strategy."

I turned next to Brian Sommer, who has been surrounded by accountants and accounting software for decades. Not only did he work for Arthur Andersen/Andersen Consulting for 18 years, but he also has many close relatives in the profession. Sommer has testified before the U.S. Treasury Department's Pathways Commission about the future of the accounting profession. He has been a keynote speaker at numerous American Accounting Association, AICPA, and ERP/financial accounting software events. Sommer is also a consultant to accounting firms, advising them on matters related to emerging technologies, sales methods, marketing, and accounting software.

Sommer's view on the accounting profession:

> "There's an old joke that goes, when 'innovation' and 'accounting' are used in the same statement, a jail term may be implied. This profession is not known for rushing out to embrace change. As of 2016, fewer than 10% of accounting firms have taken on a CRM initiative.[88] Another study in 2011 by NetProspex showed that the accounting profession

---

[88] "CRM in Accounting: The Tide Turns?", *Customer Relationship Management*, Danny Estrada, March 2016, pg. 48

was tied for fifth from the bottom as a profession least likely to use social media.[89]

However, change is coming to the profession, though at an interesting pace and manner. There are practitioners and academics who are embracing new technologies that use machine learning, Big Data, and analytics to better detect fraud, corrupt practices, insider trading, and other events with far greater speed and at a lower cost than more traditional human-powered methods.

Blockchain technologies could bring a degree of control, oversight, and risk management over transactions that was not possible in the past. Businesses will be able to verify that a given transaction and its monetary effects are absolutely valid via the unique keys used in blockchain-driven events. Each new transaction must be 'chained' to the previous transaction via a unique key with content that is tied to the previous transaction. These technologies make it exceptionally difficult and expensive for fraud to occur. If widely implemented in the next few years, blockchain technology reduces the transaction testing aspects of auditing and shifts the focus to assessment of unusual, infrequent, or one-off transactions like a capital restructuring. In essence, blockchain technology could be a force that reduces the need for lots of new college graduates in accounting firms."

Sommer then talked about the conservative nature of the profession and its resistance to change the business model:

"But, as an industry, accountants don't handle change well or quickly. They like to dissect every potential change, be it a new FASB [Financial Accounting Standards Board] accounting rule proposal or a new technology. The automatic reaction to any potential change is to not change but instead

---

[89] Source: http://mwj.bulldogsolutions.com/content/article082011_social_industries

go into 'study' mode. This pace, often glacial in nature, was a luxury that could be humored when business, technology, and global economies also changed at a similar, slow pace. That's just not realistic anymore.

Yet, institutional barriers still try to slow down 'progress' in this industry. For example, let's look at continuous auditing. To an external auditor, continuous auditing could be a nightmare scenario. If such smart technology could check almost every transaction in near-real-time, why would you need an external auditor? If an external auditor had a technology that could audit every transaction, would the auditor be legally culpable for any missed fraud? Auditors have maintained for eons that fraud detection is not the purpose of an audit. That defense worked when all they did was sample a few transactions but that 'out' may be going away.

But that risk is nothing compared to the damage automated, continuous auditing could do the auditor's business model. Many of these firms are designed around hiring piles of recent college graduates who will learn their clients' businesses and accounting issues via the conduct of audit work. If systems do this work, would accountancies need all of these new graduates? No. Worse, without the billable hours that a bunch of cheap staff auditors generate, auditing firms would also need to rethink their pyramidal staffing/ income models, training programs, and partner development tracks.

Another business model issue for accounting firms is their tendency to avoid investments. Many accounting firms are long-lived partnerships. In that structure, partners must provide the capital required to equip staff, acquire office space, etc. It also takes capital to invest in new technology and develop applications like auditing software. Such capital infusions often come at the cost of paying diminished partnership earnings/distributions. Partners that are close to retirement want to maximize current year earnings and not invest back in a firm where they will likely have no further ownership stake. The ownership and the capital structure of accounting firms may actually act as a barrier to innovation. However, it won't stop clients from adopting or pushing for these new innovations and technologies."

Sommer then focused on how the nature of accounting work is likely to evolve:

"Clerical accounting work is already going away, and it's not coming back. What will be needed are the smart accountants who possess expert knowledge and must make a number of judgment calls regarding nonstandard, one-off, or unusual transactions. The demand for such expertise is not going away.

Likewise, there will be continued demand for accountants who understand accounting policies of an acquired firm, and are able to determine how any differences can be reconciled with the parent company's books. This skill set is not an entry-level accounting function—it's for seasoned accountants. New technology will not replace such skills.

Some tax strategies may get automated, but others won't. While consumers and small businesses can use low-cost, generalized tax preparation software like TurboTax, the actual devising of complex tax strategies is still a people-intensive activity.

Businesses will need skills to double-check the details of algorithm-based and AI-based accounting technologies. The implication for controllers and CFOs is that their team may be mis-staffed from a skills perspective. Instead of having all CPAs and accounting clerks in their accounting organizations, these leaders may need people with different backgrounds in statistics, data science, analytics, algorithms, and social sciences.

The biggest challenge to the profession may not be in job losses but in what academics teach new accounting students. In a 2015 list of the top 25 technologies that practitioners and academics believe accounting students should know prior to graduating, the number one skill was in electronic spreadsheets (e.g., Microsoft Excel). Other skills that made the list included database management software, ERP software, etc. While there were some topics of current relevancy (e.g., business intelligence and analytics technologies), the list contained too many technologies of a prior, slower-paced, industrial-age world and not of today's digital economy. Newer technologies (e.g., social sentiment analysis) didn't make the list at all. If accounting curricula are rooted in a 1990s-era mindset, how will students be relevant when they graduate and stay relevant throughout their career?"

There you have it. While the good Oxford professors consider accountants and auditors very susceptible to automation, a number of cultural, legal, and other factors are making that transition slow.

Driverless Cars: Not so Fast!

Let's next turn to commercial drivers and the potential impact of autonomous vehicles. The Oxford professors calculated that truck, bus, and taxi drivers all had susceptibility scores over 0.79.

This aligns with GM's road map to autonomy. As a GM executive told *BusinessWeek*,[90] it sees an evolution starting with "driver in charge" in 2010, progressing to "driver mostly in charge" in 2015, to "car mostly in charge" in 2020, and finally "car in charge" in 2025.

There are powerful indicators that humans should not drive. In the U.S. alone, there are over 30,000 car-crash fatalities each year. Globally, over a million people die in car accidents every year.

---

[90] http://www.bloomberg.com/features/2015-gm-super-cruise-driverless-car/

Chris Urmson, former head of Google's self-driving car project, spoke at the SXSW event in Austin, TX in 2016.[91] He presented data from the six years of his project, which has clocked over 1.3 million miles of self-driving experience. In his presentation, you could laugh at some of the crazy stuff drivers and pedestrians do and face on U.S. roads. Over at YouTube, there is an entire meme on the insanity of Russian drivers. Almost every Russian car has a dash cam—as self-protection against lax and often corrupt law enforcement—and that has resulted in a rich database of videos on road behavior.

Besides citing a reduction in the number of accidents and time wasted in traffic gridlock, Urmson also pointed to the promise of less parking needed with driverless cars: "Imagine a world where the urine-scented concrete bunkers at the center of every city can be turned into residential and park space." In Los Angeles County, to take an extreme example, nearly 15% of incorporated land is dedicated to parking spaces or structures.

But GM's 2010 starting point does not accurately represent the transition from man to machine in the driving role. Machines have been taking over driving for decades. Chrysler first introduced cruise control to the masses in 1958 and in 1992, Mitsubishi introduced the LIDAR-based distance detection system, a building block of many of today's driverless prototypes. In 1999, Mercedes introduced Distronics assistive cruise control to the world. The DARPA-funded Grand Challenges for driverless cars were first held in 2004.

Similarly, at the other end of its spectrum, GM's 2025 "car in charge" projection may be too ambitious.

There are many scenarios to consider. We may have to start with tightly controlled settings—in a planned city like Masdar in the Middle East, in lightly traveled parts of New Zealand, in disciplined corridors in places like Singapore, on large farms where driverless tractors are already showing up, or in a truck platoon

---

91 https://www.youtube.com/watch?v=Uj-rK8V-rik

(where there's a human driver in the lead or middle of a train of driverless trucks). Or, it could be in a country like China, with its massive killjoy traffic jams and where the government can more easily mandate deployment.

Jim McBride, technical leader in Ford's autonomous vehicles team, had even more scenarios in an interview with ZDNet:

> "It could be as simple as, 'Downtown London is too congested and we're going to shut that off to everything apart from some mobility shuttles.' That's a different problem to saying, 'I'm going to do a ride-sharing service,' which is a different problem to saying, 'I'm going to do parcel delivery and a fleet service' or 'I'm going to do personal ownership, where you own and operate the car' . . . Each of those different uses comes with a different business model and a different time to launch it."[92]

McBride did not mention another potential scenario—a world of "flying cars." Don't scoff, as a number of prototypes are being worked on for vertical take-off and landing vehicles which may become attractive if road infrastructure takes too long to evolve to handle driverless cars.

BusinessWeek described early experiments with truck platooning in Europe, and reported that manufacturers expect platooning to start taking off in 2020:

> "Drivers will still be needed—by law they'll have to keep their hands on the wheel. But letting the rig do some of the work will result in less passing, quicker braking, and fuel savings of about 10 percent for the following trucks and a smaller gain for the lead vehicle, according to Daimler. And it will help reduce congestion. When a human is at the

---

[92] http://www.zdnet.com/article/ford-self-driving-cars-are-five-years-away-from-changing-the-world/?tag=nl.e539&s_cid=e539&ttag=e539&ftag=TRE17cfd61

wheel, a truck in some countries must maintain a distance of about half a football field from the vehicle in front of it to stop safely in an emergency. With automation, that distance shrinks to about 50 feet."[93]

I asked a trucking industry executive if requiring drivers in the following vehicles would reconcile with the significant driver shortage the industry faces. His response was that it would not entirely solve the problem but would allow them flexibility to rotate drivers and reduce some of the negatives of today's job.

While driverless technology is evolving nicely, the infrastructure—roads, legalities, etc.—needs to also develop. Delphi, an auto parts manufacturer, took its driverless vehicle on a cross-country trip in 2015. It found that pavement markings are quite different across states in spite of uniform standards.

Consumer Reports provided similar feedback:

"We were among the first to use Tesla's 'AutoPilot'—a semi-autonomous system that enables the Model S to steer itself to stay in its lane. While we found it useful on the highway, we found that it struggled on secondary roads with unclear lane markings. We cautioned that in those situations, the system should not allow itself to be operated. With a software update earlier this year, Tesla made changes to restrict its use on residential roads and roads without a center divider—a move in the right direction."[94]

This recommendation follows the Southwest Airlines philosophy of keeping pilots alert and skilled by making them fly

[93] http://www.bloomberg.com/news/articles/2016-04-22/convoys-of-automated-trucks-set-to-point-way-to-driverless-cars
[94] http://www.consumerreports.org/car-safety/tesla-fixes-self-parking-feature-after-consumer-reports-raises-safety-concern/

takeoffs and landings by hand rather than rely on autopilot computers. Even as the airline has adopted automation in the form of Required Navigation Performance (RNP), the *Wall Street Journal* reported, "Southwest says it has still retained lots of hand-flying in its procedures to keep skills sharp. One example: Instead of using computer-driven systems for landings in very low visibility as most airlines do, Southwest has a military-like 'head's up' screen—a piece of glass that folds down in front of the captain's eyes and displays navigation guidance—in its planes where the captain hand-flies even in the worst weather."[95]

The "partial automation" in autos may be comforting to some, but it scares others. According to Donald A. Norman, professor and director of the Design Lab at UC San Diego:

> "The more reliable the automation, the less likely the driver will be to respond in time for corrective action. Studies of airline pilots who routinely fly completely automated airplanes show this (as do numerous studies over the past six decades by experimental psychologists). When there is little to do, attention wanders. How long does it take a non-attentive driver to detect a problem, analyze it and respond? Note that at 60 mph a car travels 90 feet per second. In aviation, when unexpected incidents occur it can take tens of seconds for well-trained pilots to respond, sometimes minutes to figure out what to do. But an airplane is high in the sky: the pilots are well trained and have several minutes of time. In the automobile, drivers are not nearly as well-trained, yet may have to respond in seconds."[96]

---

[95]   http://www.wsj.com/articles/SB10001424052702303338304575155813404043090
[96]   http://www.sandiegouniontribune.com/news/2015/sep/26/ready-or-not-the-fully-autonomous-car-is-coming/?#article-copy

The Tesla AutoPilot feature will likely see much more scrutiny after a fatality was reported in May 2016. *Fortune* reported:

> "This was the first death of its kind, and while it's first and foremost a tragic loss of life, it also points to an array of challenges, ethical conundrums, and unanswered questions about the quest for self-driving cars. What had been theoretical debates are suddenly starkly real."[97]

Popular Mechanics, reacting to the Tesla incident, pointed out other examples of failures with "driver assist" technologies:

> "Once while driving in L.A., I intervened when Volvo's Pilot Assist tried to follow a Scion xB up an off-ramp like a wayward puppy wandering after a scent. I've had Lincoln's automated perpendicular parking system attempt to back into a spot that was already occupied. And I've lost count of the lane-keeping systems that canceled their assistance after deeming me insufficiently involved. That's the paradox of the handoff. 'Say, you haven't touched the steering wheel for 15 seconds, so I'm going to quit helping you steer. Let's hope you notice!'"[98]

While car technology continues to improve, our roads will need to significantly evolve. Traffic lights and other transportation infrastructure will have to become smarter, with sensors and lots more fiber optics, to be able to communicate with the new cars. Construction workers and traffic police will need devices to communicate with self-driving vehicles. This new investment will be needed just as cities and counties struggle to find alternatives to speeding fines, which could shrink in a world of automated cars.

---

[97] http://fortune.com/2016/07/03/teslas-fatal-crash-implications/
[98] http://www.popularmechanics.com/cars/hybrid-electric/a21702/tesla-autopilot-crashes-trust/

Let's not forget that incumbent interests will not exactly roll over. The $200 billion a year auto insurance business, the $300 billion auto aftermarket industry, and the $100 billion parking industry will continue to evolve their offerings for human-driven cars. Besides, laws will need to evolve. The insurance industry will continue to assign blame based on analysis of "who's at fault." If algorithms are to blame, product liability definitions will have to be expanded.

But the biggest resistance may come from drivers themselves. Mazda, for example, is counting on our continued love for what it has branded "Zoom-Zoom." As *Time* said, "There is no 'right to drive' enshrined in the U.S. Constitution, but forced to choose, a lot of people would rather take the wheel than the Fifth."[99] Even Steve Wozniak, cofounder of Apple, who is bullish on driverless cars, said: "I still think people will want to own a beautiful car even if you never see it . . . Look at the music industry, you used to buy your own CDs and vinyl, and I still have problems giving that up. I still want to buy them and keep them with me in a local form and not just have them in the cloud."[100]

Whereas our young are less enamored of cars than previous generations—statistically, a lower percentage of 16-year-olds are showing up for their learner's permits—the U.S. had its best year ever for car sales in 2015. (Most carmakers, however, are planning for the industry's business model to shift from units sold to miles traveled. That makes sense as autonomous cars will likely drive many more miles in their lifetimes than personally owned vehicles, many of which—like Tony DiBenedetto described in Chapter 5—are used less than 5% in any given day.)

And here's the final boost for driven cars: All the software and sensors that carmakers are embedding in vehicles are making *every* new car safer. Today, few of us have the 35 "driver assist" features that Audi offers in its Q7 SUV, but over the next few

---

[99] http://timereaders.web.fc2.com/20165a.html
[100] http://www.cio.com.au/article/598168/steve-wozniak-ai-will-eliminate-car-ownership/

years they will come to many more human-controlled models. Indeed, Honda's newest Civic LX, equipped with an advanced driver assistance system, navigated a 25-mile Detroit area road course nearly hands-free. With price points starting at a little over $20,000, it may be "driverless enough" for many customers.

While it stands to reason that many of the elderly would look forward to driverless cars as they further age, a study by the AAA shows that giving up driving at a late age may actually lead to cognitive difficulties. The study, Driving Cessation and Health Outcomes for Older Adults, also found these older drivers are nearly five times as likely to enter a long-term care facility compared to those who remain behind the wheel.[101]

In his SXSW presentation, Google's Urmson said driverless cars could be here in three years or 30. That's a really wide range. On this topic, Wozniak has said:

> "I thought by 2020 every manufacturer would have self-driving cars . . . but the problem is there are still a few things that humans will spot that the car doesn't. The car knows where the lanes are but doesn't know the cement wall is 1 inch to the left of this lane and might cross over into the lane. There's so many issues that humans will deal with on the fly that mean it's going to take an awful long time [before] cars will be truly self-driving, except maybe on very well-known routes."[102]

Thinking of a broader, global rollout, I was talking to a professor born in India who remarked, "Do you *ever* see driverless cars in Mumbai, which has few marked lanes, and where they'd be competing with cows, dogs, and pedestrians everywhere?" He did not even mention that driver guidance in India is often based

---

[101] https://newsroom.aaa.com/wp-content/uploads/2015/07/DrivingCessation_2015_FINALREPORT.pdf
[102] http://www.cio.com.au/article/598168/steve-wozniak-ai-will-eliminate-car-ownership/

on landmarks, rather than cardinal directions. It's no wonder that India's carmakers, as they plan their own driverless versions, are testing them first in the UK and Singapore.

Not just India. Many other parts of the world will have similar challenges. Let's not forget that Oscar H. Banker was granted way back in 1940 the patent for the automatic transmission. In 1965, *Playboy* highlighted "Bye-Bye Stick Shift." Now, over 50 years later, more than half of the light cars sold outside the U.S. still have manual transmissions.

The U.S. Postal Worker

The Oxford study pegged "postal mail carrier" at 0.69 and "postal service clerks" at 0.95 for susceptibility to automation. Of course, many have been predicting the death of "snail mail" for much longer as email, texting, Skype, Facetime, and social media have become our preferred methods of communicating with each other.

Yet, reports of the demise of the U.S. Postal Service have been decidedly premature. Unbelievably, the service still sorts half the world's paper-based mail and packages! Ironically, the machines and robots at the Valpak plant in St. Petersburg, FL, and the Amazon warehouses in Ruskin and Lakeland, FL, that we saw in Chapter 4, have been a veritable godsend for the U.S. Postal Service.

Over the next few years, mail delivery will change as the Postal Service looks for a new generation of vehicles to replace its existing fleet—which is, on average, 25 years old and poorly protected against the elements. The USPS is now conducting a formal RFP process, and some of the models being considered are electric and one even features a drone launcher that could drop packages on the route as the mail carrier is delivering flat mail.

USPS service clerks have been working alongside kiosks over the last decade. The kiosks are accessible 24×7 and come with a weighing scale. They allow users to process even elaborate forms of certified and return-receipt mail, to purchase stamps, and to renew P.O. boxes. The kiosks are said to be able to perform four out of five of the transactions normally handled by a retail window clerk. I, for one, find them much more convenient than waiting in line. Yet the USPS has been baffled that even after a decade, its customers have not made more use of its kiosks. An audit showed the customer adoption percentage (CAP) was 9% below their target of 35% for walk-in-capable transactions in FY 2013.[103]

No wonder, then, that the U.S. Postal Service continues to keep over 600,000 workers employed, even as it has built a marvel of automation with miles of conveyor belts, sorting machines and other technologies. These postal employees earn on average $50,000 a year, but as one of the workers told me with overtime and additional supervisory duties, he has been making over $100,000 a year. You may not always like what he delivers to your mailbox, but somebody is paying for the mailman to continue to show up, come rain or come shine.

> Let's next look at why it takes a long time for automation to completely decimate a category of jobs. We call them "circuit breakers to overautomation."

---

[103] http://www.postal-reporter.com/blog/oig-customers-not-using-usps-self-service-kiosks-as-anticipated/

CHAPTER 8

Circuit Breakers to Overautomation

↷

So, why do job curves not follow computing power curves? Why is there no "Moore's Law" which shows reliably how jobs might shrink as computing accelerates? Let's next explore the speed bumps.

The Hype Cycle of Automation

My former Gartner colleague, Jackie Fenn, wrote the following about her book, *The Technology Hype Cycle*:

> "It happens over and over again. Some innovation (a new product, a management trend) comes along that captures the public's imagination. Everybody joins the parade with great fanfare and high expectations. This 'next big thing' promises to transform the companies that adopt it—and inflict great peril on those that don't. Then, when the innovation fails to deliver as promised immediately, everyone starts bailing out. Investments are wasted; stock prices plunge; disillusionment sets in."[104]

---

[104] http://www.amazon.com/Mastering-Hype-Cycle-Innovation-Gartner/dp/1422121100/ref=sr_1_1?ie=UTF8&qid=1462906635&sr=8-1&keywords=technology+hype+cycle

Gartner's website[105] illustrates how hype cycles unfold across many technologies with their distinctive five phases in Figure 8.1. When it comes to what it calls "smart machines," Gartner says cognitive computing and smart robots are on the rise, in the left of the curve; autonomous vehicles are at the Peak of Inflated Expectations, and speech recognition is entering the Plateau of Productivity.

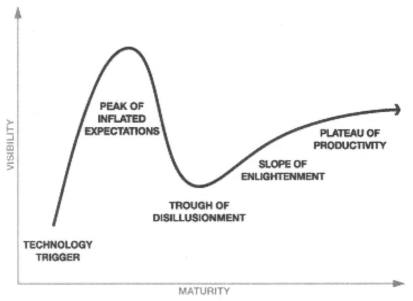

Figure 8.1   Credit–Gartner

The problem is that Gartner's depictions are taken at a particular point in time, and if you plotted the technologies' evolution over decades you would see a "camel with multiple humps." My friend Peter Fingar, who wrote a book on cognitive computing in 2014, described it thus:

> "This book is a concise report on the most noteworthy developments in artificial intelligence, a field of endeavor that's been around since the 1950s. But now, with a breakthrough

---

[105] https://www.gartner.com/doc/3099920

called 'deep learning,' artificial intelligence is finally getting human-like intelligence. The AI redux, Cognitive Computing, is having a transformational impact on work and society as a whole."[106]

Since the 1950s! That is when Alan Turing defined his famous test to measure a machine's ability to exhibit intelligent behavior equivalent to that of a human. In 1959, we got excited when Allen Newell and his colleagues coded the General Problem Solver. In 1968, Stanley Kubrick sent our minds into overdrive with HAL in his movie, *2001: A Space Odyssey*. We applauded when IBM's Deep Blue supercomputer beat Grandmaster Garry Kasparov at chess in 1997. We were impressed in 2011 when IBM's Watson beat human champions at Jeopardy! and again in 2016 when Google's AlphaGo showed it had mastered Go, the ancient board game. Currently, we are so excited about Amazon's Echo digital assistant/home automation hub and its ability to recognize the human voice, that we are saying a machine has finally passed the Turing Test. Almost.

Talking about speech recognition, Dr. Blum (whom we heard from in Chapter 1) spoke about how well it has evolved to support transcription in healthcare—but as many have found when we have asked the iPhone's "Siri" for information while driving, she still cannot overcome ambient noise, poor network connectivity, and our accents. Machines have progressively become better at understanding spoken words, but until we can get accuracy at 99%, and response times under a couple of seconds, they will continue to frustrate us. (Talking of frustration, need I mention auto-correct when you use the keyboard on your mobile phone?) To train its machines to keep improving accuracy, Google had to train its machines using messages left by users of its Voice service. Amazon's Echo constantly listens for voices (but only transmits

---

[106] http://www.mkpress.com/CC/

them for processing when a "wake word" like "Alexa" is used). Both have naturally raised questions about privacy.

We keep making progress, and yet there is so much farther to go. As IBM executive Vijay Vijayasankar wrote on his Facebook page:

> "To the world that worries about AI, machine learning and assorted algorithms becoming our overlords—I present to you . . . . LINKEDIN! A trained monkey will pick better job recommendations than what LinkedIn manages to send me in these emails."

Yann LeCun, director of AI research at Facebook, has commented, "Despite these astonishing advances, we are a long way from machines that are as intelligent as humans—or even rats. So far, we've seen only 5% of what AI can do."[107]

Matsubara, introduced in Chapter 2 and who has been training computers to write fiction, acknowledges that in today's AI-generated fiction, 80% of the creative process is actually handled by humans. He said, "AI can learn the traits of creators from past data, so if they get access to a lot of data, they can produce works resembling the original creators. Whether AI can spawn geniuses like Picasso or Nobel laureates, it's hard to say."[108]

Similarly, Yale computer science professor David Gelernter thinks we have only scratched the surface. In his book *The Tides of Mind*, he calls it "the spectrum of consciousness," which is "essentially a range of mental states through which all humans cycle each day. The cyclical element is crucial and underlies his metaphor of tidal motion. At the upper end of the spectrum, mental high tide, we are focused on the outer world, biased towards logical and abstract reasoning, and more likely to remember our

---

[107] http://www.wsj.com/articles/whats-next-for-artificial-intelligence-1465827619?href=&utm_content=buffer16d54&utm_medium=social&utm_source=facebook.com&utm_campaign=buffer
[108] http://www.japantimes.co.jp/news/2016/06/19/national/science-health/japanese-researchers-take-artificial-intelligence-toward-the-final-frontier-creativity/#.V2qJwvkrJD9

experiences later. But as we drift down through the middle and into the lower reaches of the spectrum, we become increasingly conscious of the inner worlds of memory, prefer narrative to logic, and cross eventually into the difficult-to-remember realms of dreams."[109]

We still don't understand much about the lower reaches of that spectrum. More concerning, *Time* wrote, ". . . Gelernter is vastly outnumbered—so much so that he worries that his ideas might simply be ignored. 'There has never been more arrogance and smugness' than in today's self-congratulatory scientific culture, he asserts."[110]

It's the same hype with robots. The first humanoid robot appeared in Japan in 1928. It could do simple motions like move a pen with its right hand. Today, Japan is the leading maker and consumer of robots, accounting for half of the world's production. Naturally, it has the world's largest concentration of robot engineers. Yet, these world-leading experts have tried for five years following the Tohoku earthquake to use robots to clean the radiation at the Fukushima nuclear plant. So far, all the robots sent into the reactors have failed to return.

Forget nuclear clean up—how about tidying your hair? David Bruemmer, president and CTO of 5D Robotics. describes how intimidating a hairdresser's job looks to a robot

> "Her job was really, really hard. She had to take hopelessly vague tasking like: "Give me a George Clooney haircut but kind of a bit more fun and crazy." What does that mean? I can pretty well guarantee that a robot won't ever know what that means. Regardless of trying to understand the semantics, a much harder task is figuring out how many small scissor cuts will result in an emerging look. Cutting

---

[109] http://www.chicagotribune.com/lifestyles/books/ct-prj-tides-of-mind-david-gelernter-20160224-story.html
[110] http://time.com/4236974/encounters-with-the-archgenius/

hair is not an easy job; I know I could never do it. I believe it would scare any robot as well."[111]

The 2015 DARPA Robotics Challenge Finals brought together some of the most sophisticated robots in the world. However, only three out of the 23 teams managed to complete all eight tasks, such as driving and exiting a vehicle, opening and going through a door, locating and opening a valve, using a tool to cut a hole in a wall, removing an electrical plug from a socket and putting it in a different socket, traversing rubble, and climbing stairs.[112]

As we saw in Chapter 7, the driverless technology is evolving nicely—and has been for decades—but roads and laws have not, and that will slow down widespread adoption of driverless cars.

In Chapter 1 we discussed robo-advisers. Many in Silicon Valley have predicted they will replace portfolio managers as we know them. They say this when today robo-advisers handle less than $100 billion of the $20 trillion currently under management. They say this even though the robo-advisory segment has not yet faced a sustained bear market. As the *New York Times* wrote, "In most cases, investors won't be assigned to a warmblooded professional who will be on call should markets plummet, as they have done in attention-getting fashion for most of this year. Instead, customers may receive a video message via email from a well-seasoned adviser, imploring them not to panic, though they can also reach someone at the company via online chat or phone."[113]

As Fenn said, the hype happens over and over with technology: "Investments are wasted; stock prices plunge; disillusionment sets in."

---

[111] https://techcrunch.com/2016/07/23/the-assimilation-of-robots-into-the-work-force-as-peers-not-replacements/
[112] http://www.roboticstrends.com/article/why_so_many_robots_struggled_with_the_darpa_challenge
[113] http://www.nytimes.com/2016/01/23/your-money/robo-advisers-for-investors-are-not-one-size-fits-all.html?_r=0

Automation Adopters Follow a Slow Bell Curve

Geoffrey Moore's 1991 classic, *Crossing the Chasm*, is a virtual bible for technology marketers. Many a start-up has made it required reading for the whole enterprise. Here's a typical rave review of the book on Amazon:

> "This is the book that launched my career in technology and drove me to establish a more strategic approach to marketing and business. Geoffrey Moore was ahead of his time and offers priceless information on how to stand back and reevaluate your market approach. If you know nothing about business strategy or marketing OR you consider yourself an expert, Moore's models stand the test of time and give you the tools you need to not only do your job but offers the insights that can help build consensus within a company. Apply these models to your corporate and product strategy; use it as a point of discussion with other senior executives to FINALLY drive a coherent strategy. This book changed the way I think about the business of technology, it will for you too."

Lost in the marketing adulation that the book has received is a truism: Technology buyers come in bell curves (an idea popularized by sociologist Everett Rogers). The late majority and laggards often follow the innovators several years later in adopting even promising technologies. But that's the boring stuff which comes in later years. Most marketing folk concentrate on "crossing the chasm," on the left side of the curve.

Larry Downes and Paul Nunes go even further, arguing in their book *Big Bang Disruption* that Moore's model is actually too slow, especially as it comes to consumer technology:

> "But today, new products and services enter the market better and cheaper right from the start. So producers can't rely on a class of early adopters and high margins to build

up a war chest to spend on marketing to larger and later markets. For better and for worse, thanks to near-perfect market information, consumers are too savvy for that. Everyone knows right away when some new offering gets it right—or, conversely, gets it wrong."[114]

They call their adoption curve a "shark fin," an apt term as Figure 8-2 illustrates.

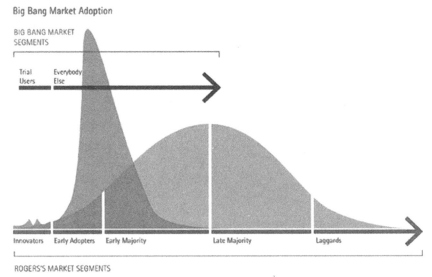

Figure 8-2   Credit: Wired

The problem is that their model does not explain the gradual, snail-like adoptions of many consumer- or individual-focused technologies.

Luther Simjian, a prolific inventor, first convinced some New York City banks in 1960 to try out his Bankograph, which was the predecessor of the modern-day ATM. But six decades later and even with mobile banking taking off, who would have thought we would still have branch banking with human tellers? According

[114] http://www.wired.com/2014/01/why-its-time-to-ditch-the-bell-curve/

to some estimates, we still have over 90,000 bank branches across the U.S., each with a cluster of tellers and other employees.

Brian Sommer, introduced in Chapter 7, pointed to me how the airline industry is having to staff up for its own version of "omni-channel".

> "Travelers frequently turn to social media to comment on every facet of their travel experiences and airlines look to technologies to sort through these missives to identify which ones warrant anything more than an acknowledgement. If it's a simple routine comment that's needed (e.g., "Yes, we're glad you got upgraded!"), then a bot gets the task. But bots cannot prevent flight cancellations, equipment failures or weather issues. The carriers still require people at the airports and on phones to re-route travelers, acquire temporary accommodations, etc. Social technologies may very well have contributed to a huge increase in the numbers of customer contacts with carriers. Using new technology allows carriers to restore some measure of balance but doesn't appear to actually allow them to cut headcount. In this instance, passengers and carriers are each deploying new technology that simply maintains stasis."

Bob Brown envisioned the e-book reader in his 1930 book, *The Readies*. In the decades since, there has been a series of readers from PARC, Sony, and others. Recently, the Amazon Kindle has allowed the digital format to really take off. Yet, printed books (and related printing, shipping, and other jobs) still account for two-thirds of all books sold in the U.S. and an even higher percentage overseas.

As the *Guardian* pointed out:

> "Kindle sales initially outstripped hardbacks but have slid fast since 2011. Sony killed off its e-readers. Waterstones last

year stopped selling Kindles and e-books outside the UK, switched shelf space to books and saw a 5% rise in sales. Amazon has opened its first bookshop. Now the official Publishers' Association confirms the trend. Last year digital content sales fell last year from £563m to £554m. After years on a plateau, physical book sales turned up, from £2.74bn to £2.76bn."[115]

As we saw in Chapter 7, Playboy magazine published an article in 1965 titled "Bye-Bye Stick Shift." Guess what? Globally, 49% of light vehicles sold in 2012 were still manual transmission.[116] In 2017, they are expected to be 46%. Outside the U.S., when you rent a car, you have to specifically ask for automatic transmission and pay a premium.

With digital voice mailboxes and most of us doing our own word processing and travel arrangements, who needs secretaries or administrative assistants? Well, according to the Bureau of Labor Statistics, that category still employs nearly four million workers.

Think travel agents have gone the way of the dodo? The BLS reports we still have 75,000 in the U.S. And around the globe many more continue to make a decent living in a world where over 40% of travel reservations are *not made* on the Internet.[117]

Who would've thunk?

One of the most innovative companies in the world with over 55,000 products, 3M keeps a close eye on new product introductions. It coined the term New Product Vitality Index (NPVI) to measure the percentage of 3M sales coming from products launched in the previous five years. In 2015, it reported its NPVI as 33.3%.[118] Bear in mind, this is one heck of an innovative company and

[115] http://www.theguardian.com/commentisfree/2016/may/13/books-ebook-publishers-paper?CMP=Share_iOSApp_Other

[116] http://www.statista.com/statistics/204123/transmission-type-market-share-in-automobile-production-worldwide/

[117] http://www.statisticbrain.com/internet-travel-hotel-booking-statistics/

[118] http://multimedia.3m.com/mws/media/1064170O/3m-2015-sustainability-report.pdf

even a product launched five years ago is considered "new." For the average company, customer adoption of its new products is considerably slower.

Take IBM, which has been talking about Watson, its cognitive computing platform, since it won the *Jeopardy!* competition in 2011. In the five years since that achievement, it has shown merely small successes in health care applications. As another friend, Evangelos Simoudis, who has long studied trends in artificial intelligence, wrote in the *Harvard Business Review*:

> "To address medium-term opportunities, IBM formed partnerships with hospitals (e.g., Memorial Sloan Kettering, The Cleveland Clinic, MD Anderson), medical device companies (Apple, Medtronic, J&J, and Novo Nordisk), and retailer CVS to develop intelligent applications on top of the Watson platform. These applications are expected to come online over the next five years. To address longer-term opportunities, IBM is investing in startups that are developing applications for the Watson platform, including Pathway Genomics and Welltok."[119]

In other words, IBM is sowing a number of seeds beyond health care (we also saw Watson starting to be used at the accounting firm KPMG in Chapter 3) but it will take years, even decades, for the platform to have a significant impact on the marketplace.

In my last book, *SAP Nation 2.0*, I tried to estimate how long SAP customers would take to adopt its newly-announced product, S/4HANA. To do so, I studied next-gen ERP product launches at J.D. Edwards, Oracle, Microsoft, and Infor going back to the early '90s, and I concluded:

> "The common thread across all the next-gen projects described in this chapter is that in the enterprise world,

---

[119] https://hbr.org/2016/02/the-5-things-ibm-needs-to-do-to-win-at-ai

new products take years to develop and then to mature. In the interim, vendors often meander or waver in their commitments. Customer bases, in turn, take decades to migrate . . . . Those are just the laws of physics. SAP may be able to bend these laws slightly with S/4, but will likely not be able to break them."

While you could argue automation technologies can provide better ROI compared to ERP systems, they follow the same rules. In fact, the long tail of Moore's bell curve is often very long, indeed.

There are many reasons for that slow adoption, and risk-averse late adopters are usually even more concerned about the security risks brought by automation. Take autonomous cars. "We are a long way from securing the non-autonomous vehicles, let alone the autonomous ones," said Stefan Savage, a computer science professor at the University of California, San Diego, at the Enigma security conference in San Francisco in early 2016. "The way modern cars are designed, once an attacker can get inside the Internet network linking the roughly 30 different computers inside, he or she can take over just about any component, from the brakes to the radio," said Savage.[120]

The U.S. FDA has warned about the risks posed by infusion pumps many hospitals use to automate IV injections:

> "Hospira and an independent researcher confirmed that Hospira's Symbiq Infusion System could be accessed remotely through a hospital's network. This could allow an unauthorized user to control the device and change the dosage the pump delivers, which could lead to over- or under-infusion of critical patient therapies."[121]

---

[120] https://www.technologyreview.com/s/546086/your-future-self-driving-car-will-be-way-more-hackable/
[121] http://www.fda.gov/MedicalDevices/SafetyandNotices/ucm456815.htm

Similarly, the U.S. FAA has been very cautious about approving nonmilitary drone usage, restricting them to the line of sight of a "pilot" on the ground. Gradually they may open up to "first person view" as goggles allow for getting a pilot-like view even on the ground. But when regulators are wary, conservative late adopters are usually even more cautious.

Incumbent Interests Conspire

Clayton Christensen is another popular author in technology circles, with books like *The Innovator's Dilemma*. His disruption theories have inspired many a start-up entrepreneur to visualize themselves as Davids against the incumbent Goliaths. The irony is that Christensen's advice is read just as avidly by incumbents as he warns them, "It is actually the same practices that lead the business to be successful in the first place that eventually can also result in their eventual demise."[122]

Most of us assume incumbent interests just roll up and die. In fact, as Chunka Mui, another thought leader, counters, "Market leaders have assets that should allow them to out-innovate almost any startup and most new entrants."[123] Market leaders have shown they can improve existing products, acquire disruptive new players, and build regulatory "moats" and other barriers to protect their interests.

Take the incumbents around autonomous vehicles. The $200 billion-a-year auto insurance and the $300 billion auto aftermarket industries will adapt and continue to market the benefits of driven cars. And what about those "concrete bunkers"—the parking structures that Google's Urmson alluded to in Chapter 7? The $100 billion parking industry is not too thrilled about autonomous cars that could move continuously and not need a space for hours. Treasurers in most cities and counties do not want to miss out on revenues from speeding tickets. They will think

---

[122] http://www.claytonchristensen.com/books/the-innovators-dilemma/
[123] http://www.forbes.com/sites/chunkamui/2016/04/25/disruption-dogma/#45ededfe3933

up alternatives, lobby, and in other ways try to protect those revenue streams.

As we discussed in Chapter 7, the biggest incumbent resistance will likely come from drivers themselves. Mazda, Porsche, and other carmakers are counting on human versus robotic drivers.

Consumers have also shown a passive-aggressive approach to most self-service automation. While some, like me, eagerly embrace self-service, many others expect a modest discount, considering that they are reducing labor costs of banks, retailers, or airlines. In fact, many are annoyed as banks tack on fees for using ATM machines and airlines charge for printing boarding passes.

This comment on an ABC News story reflects the attitude of many consumers:

> "Part of the cost of an item is to pay for the service of checkout. I'm not going to waste my time and effort, and take someone's job in the process, by checking myself out. If self checkout gave you a 5% discount on the total bill, I'd consider it, but otherwise I'd rather not take someone's job."[124]

Some customers view charges for toll tags in rental cars as taking advantage of public infrastructure they have already paid for in taxes. Avis's "convenience fee" is an example. Here's how Avis describes it: "Under the e-Toll program, once you pass through an electronic toll, you will pay a convenience fee of $3.95 for every day of the rental, including days where e-Toll is not used, up to a maximum of $19.75 per rental month, plus the incurred toll charges at the maximum rates posted by the toll authority." Hertz had to settle a class-action lawsuit accusing it of overcharging customers who (knowingly or not) used the company's "PlatePass" electronic toll "service."

---

[124] http://abcnews.go.com/blogs/technology/2012/04/self-checkout-gets-extra-set-of-eyes-with-video-software/

Other consumers roll their eyes when they receive notices from telcos to adopt electronic billing. Sure it is "green", but how about passing along some savings from the foregone printing and postage?

Some consumers resent kiosks at Home Depot and elsewhere that capture a video of their transaction. It is meant to reduce fraud, but consumers worry that their privacy is also being compromised.

How about the accounting profession that we also discussed in Chapter 7? Technology is allowing auditors to move from manual sample testing to continuous auditing—an automated review of 100% of transactions for policy violations and behavioral patterns. But, as we mentioned, accounting firms are worried about litigation if the technology misses something significant during the audit. So they are cautious about services they offer to their attest clients. They have not yet figured out a business model that does not depend on a pyramid of young staff accountants.

Dennis Howlett, introduced in Chapter 2, started his career as a chartered accountant in the UK, and uses colorful imagery to describe why he thinks the profession is ripe for a shake up:

> "Professional accountants have this idea that somehow they are Knights of the Round Table. They go into work in their shiny suits of armor and greet each other 'Good morning Sir Lancelot, good morning Sir Galahad,' and then slam down the helmet visor, disappearing into their offices to render benevolent judgment upon the day's stream of petrified clients while fighting the good fight against tax office monstrous bureaucracy. At least that's what they think they're doing."

Most accountants agree that some automation will be good for the profession, but the incumbent mindset will take a while to change, especially since they think they have a moat—regulatory protection as to who can perform an audit.

Tacit Knowledge of Workers

Hungarian-British polymath Michael Polanyi explained it succinctly: "We can know more than we can tell." In his 1966 book, *The Tacit Dimension,* he pointed out that tacit knowledge—tradition, inherited practices, implied values, and prejudgments—is a crucial part of scientific knowledge.[125]

Most knowledge management professionals talk about an iceberg that represents explicit knowledge which is relatively easy to codify and potentially automate, with a much deeper, "under-the-waterline" portion of tacit material that workers know but cannot effectively "tell."

Figure 8-3 is from Anecdote, a strategy consulting firm which helps its clients with storytelling. As the firm says, "Most of our work here at Anecdote involves working with tacit knowledge. But it is clear that there is a broad understanding about what's meant by the phrase. In the knowledge management world there are two camps: one that believes tacit knowledge can be captured, translated, converted; and the other that highlights its ineffable characteristics."[126]

---

[125] http://press.uchicago.edu/ucp/books/book/chicago/T/bo6035368.html
[126] http://www.anecdote.com/2007/08/what-do-we-mean-by-tacit-knowledge/

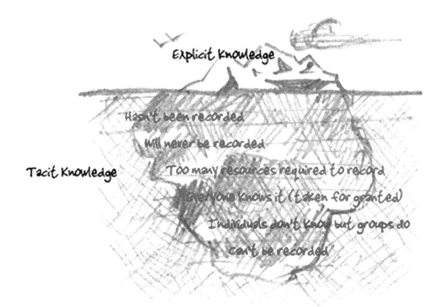

Figure 8-3   Credit: Anecdote

Many enterprises have experienced firsthand the challenge of transferring knowledge. Outsourcers often ask for months of knowledge transition time, but at least they come with methodologies for transferring institutional knowledge, even across borders. With aging workforces, however, few enterprises have systematic knowledge-transfer processes—and even when they do, the average tenure of Millennials is much shorter than that of previous generations.

On top of that, most industries have transformed over the last couple of decades, and work is now fragmented across internal staff and external providers. The McKinsey study discussed in Chapter 5 concluded:

> "According to our analysis, fewer than 5 percent of occupations can be entirely automated using current technology.

However, about 60 percent of occupations could have 30 percent or more of their constituent activities automated. In other words, automation is likely to change the vast majority of occupations—at least to some degree—which will necessitate significant job redefinition and a transformation of business processes."[127]

Mention business process transformation to many executives and they break into a cold sweat. Over the last three decades, many have lived through the chaos of process reengineering projects and ERP implementations that poorly covered many industry-specific practices.

Indeed, Mary Lacity of the University of Missouri-St. Louis and Leslie Willcocks of The London School of Economics call it "systemantics":

"One result is that workers must now spend substantial time dealing with systemantics—the quirks and shortcomings that are just as endemic to systems as their strengths. For example, it is a systemantic problem that the typical automated operations system (including Enterprise Resourcing Planning, Customer Relationship Management, e-commerce, and e-business solution systems) is unable to complete a whole process, end-to-end. For the technology to deliver value, knowledge workers must do pesky things like extract and move massive amounts of data from one system to another. Knowledge workers consistently tell us they want to be liberated from such highly-structured, routine, and dreary tasks to focus on more interesting work. Some are actually getting that wish, thanks to a new approach known as Robotic Process Automation (RPA)."[128]

---

[127] http://www.mckinsey.com/business-functions/business-technology/our-insights/four-fundamentals-of-workplace-automation

[128] https://hbr.org/2015/06/what-knowledge-workers-stand-to-gain-from-automation

Think, however, of how many RPA companies—like Automation Anywhere which we introduced in Chapter 1—would be needed to cover the breadth of the 2,000 activities across 800 occupations that are mentioned by McKinsey. And that's just to handle the software portion. Now consider the sensors, 3-D printing, and other automation technologies that would need to coalesce and allow for the vast sweep of capabilities McKinsey mentions: "from fine motor skills and navigating in the physical world, to sensing human emotion and producing natural language."

Guess who is excited about such knowledge work automation? The very consultants from Deloitte Consulting, TCS, and others who did the reengineering and ERP projects, many of them disasters, in the first place. In *SAP Nation*, I documented the massive overruns and write-offs which cost SAP customers $300 billion a year. If SAP Nation were an economy, the customer spend would rank high in a GDP listing of nations.

And if knowledge automation is so promising, why are these consultants not adopting it for their own people-intensive operations? Similar to the accountants we discussed in Chapter 7, these firms depend on pyramids of young consultants.

Some outsourcers are indeed preparing for this future. Wipro is using machine learning algorithms to help with its internal help desk support. The firm has now created an AI platform called HOLMES that uses computer algorithms to reduce human effort in many of its customers' industries. Tata Consultancy Services is working on an AI platform called ignio to help build applications quickly and get more out of its infrastructure management capability. Infosys has announced a major investment in automation capabilities as well.[129]

However, given how labor-intensive these firms are, such automation efforts will only have a tiny impact. A few good operations research experts could easily reduce the insane amount of travel endured by their staff. In *SAP Nation*, I estimated such firms

---

[129] http://blogs.wsj.com/cio/2015/07/01/bringing-outsourcing-back-to-machines/

annually cost their customers $6 billion in travel costs. (That's just around SAP projects. Now add similar amounts around Oracle, Salesforce, and other similar ERP and CRM projects.) I did not even begin to estimate the health costs that come from such sustained, long-term travel.

Besides, the knowledge automation being promised to clients by many of these firms needs to be balanced against the reality that there's plenty of business lore that workers cannot tell. It's that knowledge which the consultants would not be able to effectively automate any time soon.

A fascinating example of tacit knowledge comes from the 5,000 "dabbawalas" in Mumbai, India. These are couriers who pick up food in lunch boxes (dabbas) from the homes of customers and deliver them by train, bicycles, and carts to offices, so the spouse (or other recipient) can enjoy a hot meal. They then reverse the logistics, and deliver the 200,000 tiffin boxes back home. Even though the technology is basic, they have a remarkable, Six Sigma track record—estimated to miss one delivery in every six million.

A *Harvard Business Review* article about them said:

> "Amazingly, the dabbawalas—semiliterate workers who largely manage themselves—have achieved that level of performance at very low cost, in an ecofriendly way, without the use of any IT system or even cell phones.
>
> The dabbawala service is legendary for its reliability. Since it was founded, in 1890, it has endured famines, wars, monsoons, Hindu-Muslim riots, and a series of terrorist attacks. It has attracted worldwide attention and visits by Prince Charles, Richard Branson, and employees of Federal Express, a company renowned for its own mastery of logistics."[130]

---

[130] https://hbr.org/2012/11/mumbais-models-of-service-excellence

Their success has attracted a series of potential disrupters. *BusinessWeek* wrote:

> "More than 400 food delivery apps started up in India over the past three years, raising $120 million from venture capital firms and other investors . . . . The new services offered something dabbawalas don't: last-minute ordering and the ability to choose dishes from hundreds of restaurants . . . . Even so, most of the high-tech startups have foundered, and dozens have closed."[131]

Clearly, the dabbawalas have tacit knowledge that the smartest investors and entrepreneurs have not—yet—been able to duplicate.

The Law of Unintended Consequences

Read *Electronic House* magazine and you see fancy home theaters, electronic shades, and elaborate security systems. The massive sports industry can cite a number of technologies that make nighttime baseball or soccer possible, and that also allow games to be broadcast live around the world. But hardly anyone in the housing or sports world today bothers to credit the lawnmower. Without that humble machine, patented in 1830, we likely would not have created millions of suburban homes with their lush lawns or thousands of baseball diamonds. Without that well-manicured grass, we may well not have innovated modern irrigation systems or Astroturf or elaborate new stadium designs.

Economic history is rife with examples of small inventions with significant ripples and unintended consequences. In Chapter 7, we saw that UPC codes have led to increased store sales and many new applications like QR codes. Jobs increased, and certainly did not die. Similarly, email and e-commerce did not kill the U.S.

---

[131] http://www.bloomberg.com/news/articles/2016-02-03/india-food-apps-haven-t-replaced-traditional-dabbawalas-on-bikes

Postal Service, but rather created a new category of jobs around Sunday and same-day delivery.

Bear in mind that somebody will need to manufacture and repair today's robots and drones, code the machine learning, update the infrastructure needed to communicate with autonomous vehicles, and much more.

James Bessen, economist and a lecturer at the Boston University School of Law, pointed out:

> "Automation reduces the cost of a product or service, and lower prices tend to attract more customers. Software made it cheaper and faster to trawl through legal documents, so law firms searched more documents and judges allowed more and more expansive discovery requests. Likewise, ATMs made it cheaper to operate bank branches, so banks dramatically increased their number of offices. So when demand increases enough in response to lower prices, employment goes up with automation, not down. And this is what has been happening with computer automation overall during the last three decades. It's also what happened during the Industrial Revolution when automation in textiles, steel-making, and a whole range of other industries led to a major increase in manufacturing jobs."[132]

In the next chapter we will explore how new jobs will blossom over the next few decades as today's "lawnmowers" mature.

---

[132] http://www.theatlantic.com/business/archive/2016/01/automation-paradox/424437/#article-comments

CHAPTER 9

Gradually, then Suddenly?

↷

In Ernest Hemingway's *The Sun Also Rises,* one of the characters is asked how he went bankrupt. He responds, "Two ways. Gradually, and then suddenly." Many say we have moved to the "suddenly" phase in the demise of the human role in the labor economy.

Half Empty?

Many pessimists about automation say the exponential growth in computing power is about to lead to massive job losses. They cite Nobel-Prize-winning economist Wassily Leontief, who described how horses lost out in the workforce:

> "For many decades, horse labor appeared impervious to technological change. Even as the telegraph supplanted the Pony Express and railroads replaced the stagecoach and the Conestoga wagon, the U.S. equine population grew seemingly without end, increasing sixfold between 1840 and 1900 to more than 21 million horses and mules. The animals were vital not only on farms but also in the country's rapidly growing urban centers, where they carried goods and people on hackney carriages and horse-drawn omnibuses. But then, with the introduction and spread of the internal combustion engine, the trend rapidly reversed. As engines

found their way into automobiles in the city and tractors in the countryside, horses became largely irrelevant. By 1960, the United States counted just three million horses, a decline of nearly 88 percent in just over half a century."[133]

Here's an interesting observation: The pessimistic academic and analyst sectors could use a technology refresh in their own professions. While analysts are predicting doom and gloom from automation to other sectors, they, themselves, continue with a labor-and-paper intensive model based on dated, static tools like Magic Quadrants and Waves which were designed in previous decades.

Potentially heralding a major change, a new analyst firm in April 2016 announced the following:

> "The new firm will only sell to end users. Vendor contracts will not be renewed. In a year's time, IDC could claim to be truly independent. As well as investing in the new IDC, IBM will also provide its Watson artificial intelligence system. Watson will support new research and advisory services will be around a 3-dimensional matrix (3DM) which will be accessed through the Oculus Rift virtual reality system [see pp. 20 and 52]. Clients will be taken into a virtual world of research where they will initially interact with automated Smart Analysts. Depending on their questions, clients will move seamlessly between interacting with the AI-powered Analysts and live ones. IBM's Watson system will be underpinned with database and content management technology systems from Oracle and SAP. The consortium has announced that 'Super Analysts' including Ray Wang, Phil Fersht and Fabrizio Biscotti will also be modelled for the new 'Robotic Automated Analysts,' to be called RAAs. This automation will allow IDC to dramatically increase the number of end-user clients it can serve, to provide a

---

[133] https://www.foreignaffairs.com/articles/2015-06-16/robots-are-coming

joined-up view across analyst silos and to provide multiple language support."[134]

Don't get too excited—the press release above was an April Fool's Day spoof!

Ditto for many academicians who believe MOOC (massively online open courses) will not affect them significantly. Ray Lane, introduced in Chapter 1, who sits on a couple of university boards, does not agree:

> "I am not talking Carnegie Mellon, which had close to 20,000 applicants for a class of 1,500, or Stanford which is probably twice that. They'll be fine. Stanford could charge $100,000 a year and people will pay it. It's not price sensitive. But way too many other universities are creating their own content, they're teaching in their own classrooms. So at 3,000 sites in the United States, there's a teacher creating a class in physics and teaching physics. We are moving to shared, digital models like a Khan Academy, Coursera, or Udacity."

Finally, as we saw in Chapter 8, consultants who are peddling the benefits of process automation should really be starting closer to home. Perhaps, the medicine of all these pundits should be taken with a heaping spoonful of "Doctor, Heal Thyself!"

Fortunately, for all the doomsayers about job losses, there are countervailing optimists who say we could just as easily see long-promising industries take off and create new jobs.

Half Full?

Denis Pombriant, who we heard from in Chapter 6 talking about the Kondratiev cycle, is another such optimist. In an interview, he told me:

---

[134] http://analystrelations.org/2016/04/01/vendor-consortium-will-turn-idc-into-end-user-specialist/

"It is happening right now if you know where to look. For instance, there will be lots of new jobs in construction and maintenance. But even things that we take for granted will need to be reimagined. Take the highway system. We think about driverless cars, but why don't we also think of cars that get their electricity from the roads? It can be done.

Or consider high-speed rail. Currently trains on good tracks can run at about 200 miles per hour. If trains were to begin replacing air travel (say, people just can't stand air travel any more, a distinct possibility), it could take two days to go coast to coast by rail. But if the middle of the country were to build up, roughly on both shores of the Mississippi, people and goods from each coast could meet in the middle for all kinds of things that we primarily do on the coasts now. Opening up the continent's "third coast" would require significant investment if other factors like transportation and energy infrastructures drove the decision-making. That's an example of a spin-off effect and the number of possibilities is almost limitless."

Pombriant's point about new energy infrastructure is showing up in job data: As mentioned earlier, the BLS shows that wind turbine service technicians are the fastest-growing job category, expected to grow 108% in the decade starting 2014. Also, as road and other infrastructure are upgraded to accommodate autonomous cars, significant numbers of construction jobs will be created.

Brian Sommer, introduced in Chapter 7, points to new jobs associated with the Internet of Things (IoT). He told me:

"While lots of pundits speak to the avalanche of new IoT enabled devices about to hit the market, few understand what this will do to jobs. Depending on the source, an estimated 22–75 billion internet enabled devices will be in place by 2020. The consensus estimate is around 50 billion devices. What these pundits fail to notice is that there are only 7.3 billion people on the earth right now. What happens when these devices 'phone home' and need to be repaired or their contents replenished? Where are the new workers whose job it will be to tend to these devices? Someone needs to install, maintain, remove, recondition, etc. these devices."

It's not only urban infrastructure and alternative energy that can lead to new jobs. The National Academy of Engineers[135] has identified many more "Grand Challenges"—each of which could represent an employment boom—including the following:

- Make solar energy economical.
- Provide energy from fusion.
- Develop carbon sequestration methods.
- Manage the nitrogen cycle.
- Provide access to clean water.
- Restore and improve urban infrastructure.
- Advance health informatics.
- Engineer better medicines.
- Reverse-engineer the brain.
- Prevent nuclear terror.
- Secure cyberspace.
- Enhance virtual reality.
- Advance personalized learning.
- Engineer the tools of scientific discovery.

---

[135] http://www.engineeringchallenges.org/

On its website, the NAE rousingly explains the urgent challenges facing the world's engineers in this century:

"As the population grows and its needs and desires expand, the problem of sustaining civilization's continuing advancement while still improving the quality of life looms more immediate. Old and new threats to personal and public health demand more effective and more readily available treatments. Vulnerabilities to pandemic diseases, terrorist violence, and natural disasters require serious searches for new methods of protection and prevention. And products and processes that enhance the joy of living remain a top priority of engineering innovation, as they have been since the taming of fire and the invention of the wheel.

In each of these broad realms of human concern—sustainability, health, vulnerability, and joy of living—specific grand challenges await engineering solutions. The world's cadre of engineers will seek ways to put knowledge into practice to meet these grand challenges. Applying the rules of reason, the findings of science, the aesthetics of art, and the spark of creative imagination, engineers will continue the tradition of forging a better future."[136]

Meanwhile, Ray Kurzweil believes the Singularity is near: "The Singularity is an era in which our intelligence will become increasingly nonbiological and trillions of times more powerful than it is today—the dawning of a new civilization that will enable us to transcend our biological limitations and amplify our creativity."[137]

Kurzweil also believes advances in genetics, nanotechnology, and robotics will help the physical human body evolve much faster than it has over the millennia.

---

[136] http://www.engineeringchallenges.org/challenges/16091.aspx
[137] http://singularity.com/

Even if you consider Kurzweil's ideas too far-fetched, Luke Nosek, cofounder of PayPal and the Founders Fund, thinks human intelligence is at the cusp of dramatic advances: "If we can positively affect injured or non-neurotypical brains, we may not be far from improving connections in healthy brains and enhancing intelligence in a generalized way."[138] His view is that we should be improving human capabilities to keep up with machine advances.

Lane, described above, is optimistic about the U.S. economy: "When you think productivity, skilled workers, and a large middle class, the U.S. still owns it."

However, he does think we need to embrace change, pointing to his younger days in Pittsburgh, PA:

> "People would go to the steel mill for 10 bucks an hour. Good work. Good pay. By the time the U.S. steel industry was threatened, many of the workers were making 25 bucks an hour and demanding that they make more. When they were laid off, they refused to accept that their jobs were not coming back. They should have retrained because they were still in their 30s or 40s. They wouldn't go back to vocational school and learn a new trade. I think that is very common. As long as there's revenue today, we cannot seem to see five or 10 years out."

Peter Diamandis, in his book *Abundance* (cowritten with Steven Kotler), is even more specific about future opportunities. From a *New York Times* review of the book:

> "His thesis rests on a four-legged stool. The first idea is that our technologies in computing, energy, medicine and a host of other areas are improving at such an exponential rate

---

[138] http://www.wsj.com/articles/whats-next-for-artificial-intelligence-1465827619?href=&utm_content=buffer16d54&utm_medium=social&utm_source=facebook.com&utm_campaign=buffer

that they will soon enable breakthroughs we now barely think possible. Second, these technologies have empowered do-it-yourself innovators to achieve startling advances—in vehicle engineering, medical care and even synthetic biology—with scant resources and little manpower, so we can stop depending on big corporations or national laboratories. Third, technology has created a generation of technophilanthropists (think Bill Gates) who are pouring their billions into solving seemingly intractable problems like hunger and disease. And finally, we have what Diamandis calls "the rising billion." These are the world's poor, who are now (thanks again to technology) able to lessen their burdens in profound ways."[139]

An example of Diamandis's final point is China, which now has a fifth of the global population and 10% of the global wealth. Its middle class, according to Credit Suisse,[140] is now the largest in the world.

The Flat Earth
A paper by Justin Yifu Lin of the World Bank explains the "formula" China used (italics added) and is being used as a guidebook by other emerging countries:

"After the transition was initiated by Deng Xiaoping in 1979, China adopted the opening-up strategy and started to tap the potential of *importing what the rest of the world knows and exporting what the world wants.* This is demonstrated by the rapid growth in its international trade, the dramatic increase in its trade dependence ratio, and the large inflows of foreign direct investment. While in 1979 primary and

---

[139] http://www.nytimes.com/2012/04/01/books/review/abundance-by-peter-h-diamandis-and-steven-kotler.html?pagewanted=1&_r=2
[140] http://www.telegraph.co.uk/finance/china-business/11929794/Chinas-middle-class-overtakes-US-as-largest-in-the-world.html

processed primary goods accounted for more than 75 percent of China's exports, by 2009 the share of manufactured goods had increased to more than 95 percent. Moreover, China's manufactured exports upgraded from simple toys, textiles, and other cheap products in the 1980s and 1990s to high-value and technologically sophisticated machinery and information and communication technology products in the 2000s. China's exploitation of the *advantage of* backwardness has allowed the country to emerge as the world's workshop and to achieve extraordinary economic growth by reducing the costs of innovation, industrial upgrading, and social and economic transformation."[141]

India has built impressive software capabilities over the last three decades. The majority of Fortune 500 companies work with outsourcing firms that have significant staffing in India. The Indian software/business process outsourcing industry is estimated to generate $150 billion a year and its trade body, NASSCOM, is constantly studied by development officials in other countries seeking to mirror its success.

You can criticize both China and India for their terrible pollution problems and on a variety of other points. Additionally, with a growing backlash toward globalization as seen in the "Brexit" UK vote and in the U.S. Presidential race, the Chinese and Indian model cannot continue to just export people and products. Both countries have certainly shown the ability to create millions of new jobs. Public entities like the Chinese People's Liberation Army and the Indian Railways continue to be some of the largest employers in the world, even as they modernize jobs with contemporary technologies.

These countries also show the "art of the possible" around job growth. In the West, it is nearly impossible to get approvals

---

[141] http://siteresources.worldbank.org/DEC/Resources/ChinaMiracleDemystified-Shanghai.pdf

to build a new airport or even extend runways. In China, under the 2011–2015 national plan, 82 new commercial airports were approved for construction.[142] You can laugh about the quality of Bollywood films but they are a major employer in India, and have inspired Nollywood in Lagos, Nigeria, and Chollywood in Peru.

Even more encouraging is the success of smaller countries like Singapore, Dubai, and, more recently, Estonia, all of which have managed to transition their citizens with new skills.

The small island nation of Singapore possesses few natural resources but it is a major global player in sectors such as electronics, petroleum refining, shipping, financial services, and biomedicine. The country maintains its competitive position by constantly refreshing its labor force and its educational system through a sophisticated system of planning coordinated across the Ministry of Manpower, the Economic Development Board, the Ministry of Education, other government agencies, and local businesses.

Dubai, eager to diversify from dependence on oil revenues, has become a vibrant shopping and tourist center. It has some of the best shipping and aviation infrastructure in the world. Most airports around the world still cannot accommodate the Airbus A380, the largest aircraft in the sky. But Emirates, Dubai's national carrier, has a dedicated hub able to handle the airline's 75 A380s. Dubai has also attracted "medical tourism" with its world-class health care facilities.

In *The New Technology Elite*, I had included a case study on Estonia's "Tiigrihüpe," or Tiger Leap, after decades of stagnation under the Soviet Union:

> "Having blazed a digital trail, Estonia is now poised to also lead the world on cybersecurity even as the world tries to emulate what Estonia has offered its citizens for over a decade now."

---

[142] http://www.chinadaily.com.cn/cndy/2012-11/27/content_15961024.htm

In Africa, Kenya has become a leader in mobile payments and Rwanda is becoming a testing ground for many drone-based services.

And it's not just emerging countries. Technology startup magnets around the world include Berlin's Silicon Allee, Tel Aviv's Silicon Wadi, Cambridge's Silicon Fen, Dublin's Silicon Docks, Paris's Silicon Sentier, Toronto's Discovery District, and Geneva's Health Valley.

Not Your Grandpa's Job

As companies swim with Big Data from sensors, social media, and a variety of other sources, we are seeing interesting new job patterns. Google's Chief Economist Val Harian was prescient when he said several years ago, "I keep saying that the sexy job in the next 10 years will be statisticians." [143] Statistics is the new plastics!

Ten years ago, no one would have predicted there would be millions of iOS and Android developers. Similarly, no one would have projected that Zumba instructors, pet care providers, or mobile truck food operators would be some of the fastest growing jobs in the U.S. Stop by a local Whole Foods and flip through an issue of *Natural Awakenings*, a publication which carries ads from practitioners in the growing "alternative health,care" market. This includes acupuncturists, yoga instructors, and herbalists among others. The publication claims nearly four million readers in 90 markets in North America. This represents an entire services sector that did not exist a couple of decades ago. Or review FastCompany's projection of jobs in the next decade to include Urban Farmers, Neuro-Implant Technicians, and Virtual Reality Experience Designer.[144]

---

[143] http://www.nytimes.com/2009/08/06/technology/06stats.html?_r=2& mtrref=www.conversion-rate-experts.com&gwh=F675E194B26987386B3A6E78BAA 15E7E&gwt=pay
[144] http://www.fastcompany.com/3046277/the-new-rules-of-work/the-top-jobs-in-10-years-might-not-be-what-you-expect/1

The franchise industry continues to truck along and keep nine million individuals employed in the U.S. An analysis by the International Franchise Association[145] shows the changing face of that sector. It now includes paint-and-sip studios such as Pinot's Palette and Painting with a Twist, tax franchises such as H&R Block and Liberty Tax, upscale quick-serve restaurants like Panera Bread, and commercial and residential services like Jan-Pro and ServiceMaster Clean.

Whether you are pessimistic or optimistic about automation and the labor market, we have not focused enough on an even bigger, more urgent issue—that for a while now, we have been sending confusing signals to the labor economy.

Let's explore that issue next.

---

[145] http://businessideatrends.com/the-6-best-franchise-types-for-2016/

SECTION III

Guiltless Automation

CHAPTER 10

Don't Blame
Machines for This!

∿→

While we fret about machines destroying jobs, we are less focused on the man-made damage to the labor economy. Let's explore that in this chapter.

The Dysfunctional Labor Economy

On the morning of June 3, 2016, the news was abuzz with job statistics, as the *Wall Street Journal* summarized:

> "The U.S. job market notched its weakest monthly gain in more than five years, knocking down expectations for a Federal Reserve rate increase and stirring worries about the seven-year-old economic expansion."[146]

The job report for the following month was much healthier. Few news sources, however, mentioned that for the last several months there were over five million job openings which were going unfilled—near the peak in the more than 15 years the Bureau of Labor Statistics has been tracking that metric. In reverse, others point out that "the 'official' unemployment rate doesn't count

---

[146] http://www.wsj.com/articles/u-s-added-only-38-000-jobs-in-may-1464957215

discouraged workers who have settled for part-time jobs or have given up looking altogether. Tracking those individuals, under what's called the 'U-6' rate, gives a very different measure of the nation's unemployment rate: 14.3%."[147]

The headlines should have been about the significant mismatch between employer needs and labor supply.

In Chapter 5, we had pointed to anomalies in the labor economy including out-of-control housing costs in the Bay Area, and the underutilization of women workers and digitally savvy young workers. It's clear that employers, regulators, and workers are sending and getting all kinds of confusing messages. It's like Topsy-Turvy Day in Paris, as portrayed in the Disney movie *The Hunchback of Notre Dame*, where "Every man's a king, and every king is a clown." We are not sure what to believe.

How did we get here?

The Clover-Leaf Organization

Management philosopher Charles Handy was prescient when he wrote in his 1989 book *The Age of Unreason* about the "Shamrock Organization." With Handy's Irish roots, the shamrock seemed fitting as the organization he described also had three "leaves":

- The first leaf of the shamrock was made up of key executives and professionals who possess the skills that reflect the organization's core competence.

- The next leaf was made up of project specialists who are hired on contract and paid in fees for results rather than in wages or employee benefits.

---

[147] http://www.forbes.com/sites/dandiamond/2013/07/05/why-the-real-unemployment-rate-is-higher-than-you-think/#4e6a9598368c

- The third leaf comprised the contingent work force for short periods of engagement, usually paid by the hour or day, often through temp agencies.

Other authors like Geoffrey Moore—whom we discussed in Chapter 8—have defined terms like "core" and "context" to similarly encourage managers to concentrate on segments of their business where they should be investing most of their efforts.

You could argue that if Handy had written the book today he would consider a four-leaf clover as his defining metaphor, with the fourth leaf covering machines, robots, and other automation as another source of the "talent" we saw on display in Chapters 1–5.

Actually, clovers can have many more leaves. The *Guinness World Records* says one was found with 56 leaves. If you look at all the ways organizations utilize talent these days, Handy's three leaves have many derivatives, most enabled by advances in technology.

Apple has several thousand employees who develop products which are then sold in its retail stores. Its contract manufacturer, Foxconn, employs thousands of employees and robots in its manufacturing plants in China. Those plants also have interns and other staff hired through third-party recruitment firms. Apple's third-party logistics providers like FedEx have a similar mix of man and machine. There are also millions of associated jobs that are not on Apple's payroll around the apps, music, movies, books, and other items in the Apple ecosystem. Just around apps, Apple claims to support a broad community: "Nearly three-quarters of those jobs—over 1.4 million—are attributable to the community of app creators, software engineers and entrepreneurs building apps for iOS, as well as non-IT jobs supported directly and indirectly through the app economy."[148] It also says, "The iOS app

---

[148] https://www.apple.com/pr/library/2016/01/06Record-Breaking-Holiday-Season-for-the-App-Store.html

economy has created 1.2 million jobs in Europe and 1.4 million jobs in China."

Amazon has communities of authors who publish using its Kindle Direct tools, couriers who are part of its Flex delivery ecosystem, "providers" who complete tasks in its Mechanical Turk service, and a vast range of third-party merchants who utilize its fulfillment capabilities. (According to estimates, as much as 90% of certain product categories such as patio furniture sold on Amazon, come from third parties.)

Uber calls its estimated 160,000 drivers "partners"—spread across 400 cities around the world. Airbnb has "hosts" who manage over 1.5 million properties that it lists. The partners and hosts are not employees. Rather, they use the technology platforms of these companies to connect with millions of users who use their apps for commutes and lodgings.

Even more mainstream companies use various flavors of outsourcing. Companies use contract manufacturers, third-party logistics providers, digital agencies, product-design firms, law firms, IT providers, and business process outsourcing services that are "off balance sheet"—they represent the talent in Handy's second and third leaves.

The worldwide improvement in telecommunications and aviation technology has enabled many companies to leverage global talent pools.

Most enterprises have been experimenting with customer self service via ATM machines and other kiosks, interactive voice response, mobile apps, and other technologies. It is a version of "the customer as worker"—helping them help themselves rather than depending on an employee for specific services.

Then there is the franchise model, which has come a long way since Ray Kroc built the McDonald's empire starting in the 1950s with his phrase, "In business for yourself, but not by yourself." As mentioned in Chapter 9, franchises of every flavor account for nearly nine million U.S. employees. According to an annual analysis by IHS Economics, "Employment growth in the franchise sector will continue to outpace the growth of employment in all businesses economy-wide, as it has in each of the last five years . . . The gross domestic product (GDP) of the franchise sector will increase by 5.6% to $552 billion in 2016. This will exceed the growth of U.S. GDP in nominal dollars, which is projected at 4.4%. The franchise sector will contribute approximately 3% of U.S. GDP in nominal dollars."[149]

Acceleration in the Digital Economy

The hot buzzword these days is "digital transformation." Karl-Heinz Streibich, CEO of Software AG, was ahead of the curve in describing the phenomenon with his 2013 book *The Digital Enterprise* (which I helped him narrate). In it, he said we are moving from systems of record, beyond systems of engagement, to systems of competitive advantage. As he put it:

> "The personalities and companies that contributed cases to this book are embedding technology in their products and services, moving to technology-enabled business models, and utilizing technology to redefine their distribution channels. They are implementing digital technologies in both product-facing and customer-facing areas. This is technology that helps generate revenue, that helps to improve business results for companies in their social and economic environments, and that helps public agencies provide better citizen services. In short, it helps to create a better world. Even more interesting is the fact that these examples are not localized in any one industry, such as automobiles, or in a specific region, such as Silicon Valley."[150]

---

[149] http://emarket.franchise.org/FranchiseOutlookJan2016.pdf
[150] http://www.amazon.com/Digital-Enterprise-Karl-Heinz-Streibich/dp/0989756408/ref=sr_1_1?s=books&ie=UTF8&qid=1462110673&sr=1-1&keywords=the+digital+enterpris

These digital transformations which can lead to competitive advantage are a double-edged sword, and have put executives on notice—corporate half-lives are shrinking. The *MIT Technology Review* explains:

> "Back in 1958, a company could expect to stay on the [S&P 500] list for 61 years. These days, the average is just 18 years. Companies can fall off the S&P 500 when they get too small, or get acquired. No one really knows why the rate of turnover is speeding up, but technological disruption could be one big reason. Since 2002, Google, Amazon, and Netflix have joined the S&P 500, while Kodak, the New York Times, Palm and Compaq have all been forced off, essentially by changing technology."[151]

So, with their shorter life expectancies, companies have been eager to get away from lifetime employment concepts, avoid pensions, and, increasingly, not even pay for health care.

Jeffrey Pfeffer, a professor at Stanford Business School, wrote in *Fortune*:

> "Company attempts to shed responsibility for their employees—and costs—is an old story. Many years ago, some employers decided that having actual employees was a pain. There were the payroll taxes, the expense and time of hiring, legal exposure to wrongful discharge and discrimination suits if you fired people; all in all, too much trouble. So, employers offloaded employees and their work to temporary help agencies and contracting organizations, which is one reason that 'nonstandard employment' has grown so rapidly."[152]

---

[151] https://www.technologyreview.com/s/519226/technology-is-wiping-out-companies-faster-than-ever/

[152] http://fortune.com/2014/11/24/uber-airbnb-sharing-economy-fallacy/

While the varied sources of talent described above have given most enterprises plenty of flexibility, it has made talent management an incredibly complex exercise.

The Talent Rubik's Cube

Most human resources (HR) departments struggle to keep up with even the reduced load of full-time employees and related payroll, benefits, and compliance issues. The Glassdoor site (where employees post candid reviews about employers) said on its blog:

> "Talk to anyone trying to find a job, and you'll hear the same old groans. 'Job hunting is a black hole.' 'This whole process is demoralizing.' 'I feel like I'm spinning in circles.' It's no secret that recruiting is broken. The current process leaves both parties—recruiters and candidates alike—exhausted. It's time that companies make improvements or risk damaging their brand."

Contractor budgets, in turn, are managed in other parts of the enterprise by procurement groups. These workers are often asked to deal with a third party—a "vendor management organization." This arm's-length relationship is designed to preclude contractors from claiming employee benefits. It leads, however, to even less familiarity with the contractor talent pool. In turn, contractors have to put up with substandard systems and processes at many of the external organizations, and have to pay 3% to 5% of their billings for the privilege. I have spoken to a number of small businesses who have quit servicing companies who require them to go through such entities. Still others pass along the "fee" in the form of even higher invoices.

Outsourcing arrangements are managed by individual business areas—engineering works with product-design firms, marketing with digital agencies, etc. These outsourcing arrangements are similarly convoluted. While many outsourcing firms prefer to work in project or long-term contract mode, they are often cherry-picked for short-term, supplemental staffing.

Ownership of "machines" is similarly fragmented—the plant manager likely knows about shop floor robots, and someone in IT may know how many web services or service bots are deployed, but few companies have an executive responsible for coordinating all their automation efforts.

As a result, very few organizations have a complete map of all the talent they are leveraging. That's remarkable, considering that for many companies 80% to 90% of their talent is now "off balance sheet"—not directly on their payroll.

No wonder that much "outsourced" talent leads to suboptimal returns. In the IT world that I am pretty familiar with, the move is usually justified to make labor costs variable, but usually they are repeated each year and become fixed costs which are difficult to chisel down. There are a growing number of companies like GM and AstraZeneca which have started to invert their in-house staff/outsourced staff ratio. In *SAP Nation*, I had a case study where Dave Smoley, CIO of AstraZeneca, the UK pharmaceutical company, described his charter to reduce by half their annual IT budget of $1.3 billion. The biggest payback in their case is coming from inverting the 70% outsourced model and bringing nearly 4,000 jobs back in-house.

Regulators and Talent Swings

Regulators have struggled to keep up with these workplace changes, even as they try to hold on to tax, retirement, and other revenue sources while companies shift the talent mix away from employees.

In the U.S., what used to be primarily reported to the Internal Revenue Service on W2 forms as "wages" is now splintered across form 1099—Miscellaneous Income (which is also used to report royalties and other income); Schedule C, which is used to report income or loss at a sole proprietorship; and Form 1120, which many small businesses that work for larger companies use to report their corporate income.

Another example comes from tax and other incentives as local governments and nations compete with each other to attract corporate jobs. There is growing evidence that it is a zero-sum game, or at least one that regulators do not play well. As Daniel J. Wilson at the Federal Reserve Bank of San Francisco wrote:

> "Empirical studies tend to focus on the effects of policies within a jurisdiction and not on whether they adversely affect other jurisdictions. However, when Chirinko and Wilson (2008) and Wilson (2009) addressed this question, they found the answer was roughly yes."[153]

He then asks, "Would the nation as a whole be better off if competition among local governments using taxes or incentives were banned?"

The Bureau of Labor Statistics has all kinds of occupational data. But if *Time* is correct, there is a large untracked labor economy that technology has facilitated:

> "There is no one name—whether sharing economy, gig economy or on-demand economy—that captures the diversity of this disruption. But it's clear that the demand for this way of working and consuming is profound. According to a first-of-its-kind poll from TIME, strategic communications and global public relations firm Burson-Marsteller and the Aspen Institute Future of Work Initiative, 44% of U.S. adults have participated in such transactions, playing the roles of lenders and borrowers, drivers and riders, hosts and guests. The number this represents, more than 90 million people,

---

[153] http://www.frbsf.org/economic-research/publications/economic-letter/2015/february/jobs-state-tax-incentives-economic-growth/

is greater than the number of Americans who identify, respectively, as Republicans or Democrats."[154]

The labor in this market is learning to become agile, as *BusinessWeek* noted in an article on a start-up that relies on the gig economy:

> "Unlike a typical software or app company, Doordash requires an army of workers to provide the product. Yes, such companies have managed to contract out the labor and pay no benefits. But many of their workers are short-timers who expect flexible schedules and are constantly looking for the next gig. As a result, Doordash must compete with other delivery and ride-sharing services for drivers—a recipe for high recruitment and retention costs."[155]

Indeed, talk to any Uber driver and they will likely tell you they have also tried driving for Lyft.

There is a growing clamor for "modernizing labor laws" in this changed talent market. As part of the Brooking Institution's Hamilton Project, Seth D. Harris of Cornell University and Alan B. Krueger of Princeton University (both of whom also previously held roles in the Obama Administration) propose the concept of an "independent worker":

> "New and emerging work relationships arising in the 'online gig economy' do not fit easily into the existing legal definitions of 'employee' and 'independent contractor' status. The distinction is important because employees qualify for a range of legally mandated benefits and protections that are not available to independent contractors, such as the right to organize and bargain collectively, workers' compensation

---

[154] http://time.com/4169532/sharing-economy-poll/
[155] http://www.bloomberg.com/news/articles/2016-05-24/valley-s-venture-capitalists-are-souring-on-uber-style-startups

insurance coverage, and overtime compensation. This paper proposes a new legal category, which we call 'independent workers,' for those who occupy the gray area between employees and independent contractors."[156]

The BLS is also slow in keeping up with new job definitions. Hollywood has made "horse whisperer" and "wedding planner" household names, but the BLS lumps such designations into broader categories like Animal Trainer and Meeting, Event, and Convention Planners. The BLS today classifies workers into one of 840 detailed occupations, in accordance with the 2010 Standard Occupational Classification (SOC) system. The next revision to the SOC is due in 2018, and then once a decade after that.

Once a decade in this fast-moving world?

Even more critical may be for the BLS to compile automation technologies next to each job category it tracks. In the first four chapters, we looked at how machine learning, robotics, drones, exoskeletons, and 3-D printing are transforming various jobs, but there is little statistical analysis of their ratios to humans.

Time wrote about U.S. Federal Reserve Board Chair Janet Yellen:

> "She made it clear there are plenty of things about the economy both at home and abroad that the Fed—not to mention economists, investors, politicians and the rest of us—doesn't grasp right now. Unemployment has dropped to pre-crisis levels, but wages remain stagnant. The traditional relationship between job creation and inflation seems to have broken down. More and more technology has not boosted productivity, as it has in the past. Asset classes like stocks or bonds no longer move together in the ways they used to.

---

[156] http://www.hamiltonproject.org/assets/files/modernizing_labor_laws_for_twenty_first_century_work_krueger_harris.pdf

In short, the global economy is playing by new rules, rules Yellen and the Fed itself are trying to puzzle out."[157]

Confusing Our Young Workers

The confusing signals from corporations and regulators have taken a significant toll on younger workers. Worse, many of us blame the problem on these workers themselves. The Millennial generation perplexes many organizations. The Pew Research Center explained:

> "Millennials are the most diverse adult generation: 57% are non-Hispanic whites, while 21% are Hispanic, 13% are black and 6% are Asian. Each older generation is less diverse. Non-Hispanic whites make up 61% of Generation X, 72% of Baby Boomers and 78% of the Silent generation."[158]

Millennials are also the most digitally savvy generation, a critical attribute in our "silicon collar" economy. They have other positives, as *Time* pointed out:

> "Smoking rates are starkly down, and exercise is up. More than young people in the past, millennials have friends they count on in tough times."[159]

Jordan Weissman argued in *The Atlantic* that they deserve more sympathy:

> "Every generation likes to believe that it came of age at an especially trying moment in history. Millennials have the Great Recession to lament. Gen X had the dotcom bust. The Boomers had Vietnam. And the Silents had the early Cold War, complete with the not-so-silly threat of nuclear war.

---

[157] http://time.com/4291950/janet-yellen-fed/
[158] http://www.people-press.org/2015/09/03/the-whys-and-hows-of-generations-research/
[159] http://time.com/4371185/what-millennials-already-know-about-growing-old/

But at least when it comes to the job market, I think we can all agree by now that today's young adults are deserving of at least a few extra pity points."[160]

A significant example of how we have confused this generation of worker comes from the U.S. student debt crisis, where over $1.3 trillion in student debt is owed by 40 million, mostly young adults—up more than 80% since the recession.

According to a Brookings Institute report:

> "Since 2000, there has been an upsurge in the number of 'nontraditional borrowers' attending for-profit schools and, to a lesser extent, community colleges and other non-selective institutions . . . Students who borrowed substantial amounts to attend for-profit and community college were more likely to drop out of their programs and experienced poor labor market outcomes that made their debt burdens difficult to sustain."

And yet, the report continued:

> "In 1962 one cent of every dollar spent in America went on higher education; today this figure has tripled. Yet despite spending a greater proportion of its GDP on universities than any other country, America has only the 15th-largest proportion of young people with a university education."[161]

Much of the student debt is attributed to "degree inflation." An example comes from administrative assistants, or what used to be called "secretaries." As the *New Republic* reported:

---

[160] http://www.theatlantic.com/business/archive/2014/02/indisputable-evidence-that-millennials-have-it-worse-than-any-generation-in-50-years/283752/
[161] http://www.economist.com/news/united-states/21567373-american-universities-represent-declining-value-money-their-students-not-what-it

"In 2005, according to IAAP's surveys, admins most commonly had taken some college courses but didn't have a degree, while 11 percent hadn't gotten any higher education. By 2015, they most commonly had a bachelor's degree, while less than 17 percent had some college under their belt and less than 8 percent had just a high school diploma. More than 3 percent had a Master's."[162]

Wikipedia calls it "credentialism and educational inflation":

"There are some occupations which used to require a high school diploma, such as construction supervisors, loans officers, insurance clerks and executive assistants, that are increasingly requiring a bachelor's degree. Some jobs that formerly required candidates to have a bachelor's degree, such as becoming a Director in the federal government, tutoring students, or being a history tour guide in a historic site, now require a master's degree. As well, some jobs that used to require a master's degree, such as junior scientific researcher positions and sessional lecturer jobs, now require a Ph.D. Finally, some jobs that formerly required only a Ph.D., such as university professor positions, are increasingly requiring one or more postdoctoral fellowship appointments."[163]

No wonder we have mismatches in skills. Students are committing to four, six, eight years of higher education in a specific profession. That is the opposite of the agility which corporations are demonstrating in their talent sourcing. Nor does that much investment make sense when the BLS points out, "The average person born in the latter years of the baby boom (1957–1964) held 11.7 jobs from age 18 to age 48, according to the U.S. Bureau of

---

[162] https://newrepublic.com/article/121712/slow-death-secretary
[163] https://en.wikipedia.org/wiki/Credentialism_and_educational_inflation

Labor Statistics. Nearly half of these jobs were held from ages 18 to 24."[164]

A *New York Times* investigation showed even significant retraining investments are not helping:

> "Millions of unemployed Americans like Mr. DeGrella have trained for new careers as part of the Workforce Investment Act, a $3.1 billion federal program that, in an unusual act of bipartisanship, was reauthorized by Congress last month with little public discussion about its effectiveness. Like Mr. DeGrella, many have not found the promised new career. Instead, an extensive analysis of the program by The New York Times shows, many graduates wind up significantly worse off than when they started—mired in unemployment and debt from training for positions that do not exist, and they end up working elsewhere for minimum wage."[165]

Not Much Better for the Older Worker, Either

At the other end of the generational bell curve, we saw in Chapter 5 that with pensions disappearing, aging workers need to stay on jobs much longer, and by doing so are squeezing out younger workers.

Many organizations only grudgingly continue with aging workers because they are considered more "expensive" than younger workers. However, a 2015 study conducted by Lincolnshire, IL-based Aon Hewitt found that "recruiting workers age 50 and older increases a company's total labor costs by 1 percent or less, while retaining them results in an increase of 1 to 2 percent."[166]

---

[164] http://www.bls.gov/news.release/pdf/nlsoy.pdf
[165] http://www.nytimes.com/2014/08/18/us/workforce-investment-act-leaves-many-jobless-and-in-debt.html?_r=1
[166] http://www.humanresourceexecutive-digital.com/humanresourceexecutive/june_2016__2?sub_id=EtyG2t48sjIy&folio=14&pg=16#pg16

Not surprisingly, a Pew Research Center survey showed a discontented adult workforce, and one that some politicians are tapping into:

> "And although 11% of today's workers are at least somewhat concerned that they might lose their jobs as a result of workforce automation, a larger number are occupied by more immediate worries—such as displacement by lower-paid human workers, broader industry trends or mismanagement by their employers."[167]

While the shocking "Brexit" vote for Britain to leave the EU was widely seen as a backlash to globalization, there was another nuance. Aging workers showed their discontent. According to an exit poll, 56% of citizens aged 50 to 64 and 61% of those over 65 voted to leave. In contrast, 75% of citizens between 18 and 24 voted to remain.[168]

The Added Complexity of Globalization

An apocryphal tale is told about Henry Ford II showing Walter Reuther, the veteran leader of the United Automobile Workers union, around a newly automated car plant. "Walter, how are you going to get those robots to pay your union dues," gibed the boss of Ford Motor Company. Without skipping a beat, Reuther replied, "Henry, how are you going to get them to buy your cars?"[169]

Whether that tale is true or not, we are seeing a similar impact of global talent sourcing on the U.S. economy. Economist Paul Craig Roberts wrote in *How the Economy Was Lost: The War of the Worlds*:

---

[167] http://www.pewinternet.org/2016/03/10/public-predictions-for-the-future-of-workforce-automation/?utm_content=buffer548c4&utm_medium=social&utm_source=twitter.com&utm_campaign=buffer
[168] http://www.politico.eu/article/britains-youth-voted-remain-leave-eu-brexit-referendum-stats/
[169] http://www.economist.com/blogs/babbage/2011/11/artificial-intelligence?fsrc=scn/tw/te/bl/ludditelegacy

"The loss of tax base has threatened the municipal bonds of cities and states and reduced the wealth of individuals who purchased the bonds. The lost jobs with good pay resulted in the expansion of consumer debt in order to maintain consumption."[170]

In addition to the impact of global trade, the impact of immigration on labor pools is increasingly under scrutiny. The U.S. has had a quota of a million *legal* immigrants a year over the last few decades. However, the majority of these immigrants are admitted based on family reunification, not talent. They are the spouses or parents of talent-based immigrants. Instead of giving preference to talent, we have added new "lanes"—H-1B, L-1, and other types of "temporary" visas, or in the case of the agriculture and construction sectors, have allowed a flow of undocumented aliens. Next, the annual H-1B limit that the government announces is allowed to be exceeded with an uncapped flow of nonprofit and governmental researchers. Students on F-1 visas enrolled in STEM (science, technology, engineering, and math) fields of study from accredited educational institutions in the U.S. are allowed to work for as long as three years as part of "practical training."

The Center for Migration Studies, a New York City think tank, estimates we have 10.9 million undocumented workers. Many others believe we really do not have a good handle on how large that number is. The politicians keep talking about "comprehensive immigration reform" and "building walls," but the flow continues. Even for a country of immigrants, this has been unpalatable to the general population. What has been a competitive advantage for the U.S.—smart, talented immigrants—is increasingly at risk from a populist backlash.

---

[170] http://www.amazon.com/How-Economy-Was-Lost-Worlds/dp/1849350078

Skills mismatches are not just common in the U.S. An OECD report summarized:

> "Skill mismatches and shortages are common in advanced economies. Many workers believe they have the skills to cope with more demanding work while some think they need more training to cope well with duties. On average, more than 40% of European workers feel their skill levels do not correspond to those required to do their job, with similar findings for Mexico, Japan and Korea. In parallel, many employers report that they face recruitment problems due to skill shortages. Some degree of misalignment between the supply and demand for skills is inevitable, particularly in the short run. However, the costs of persistent mismatches and shortages are substantial. For instance, skill shortages can constrain the ability of firms to innovate and adopt new technologies while skill mismatches reduce labour productivity due to the misallocation of workers to jobs. Individuals are also affected as skills mismatch can bring about a higher risk of unemployment, lower wages, lower job satisfaction and poorer career prospects."[171]

The *New York Times* wrote about labor protests in France:

> "It may seem that the French are constantly on strike, or dealing with one. Yet overlooked in all the chanting, banner waving and tire burning is that the strike in France today is often a carefully choreographed dance between labor, government and the public and it is just the latest chapter in a 132-year tradition, dating from the founding of the country's first trade unions in 1884.

---

[171] http://www.keepeek.com/Digital-Asset-Management/oecd/employment/getting-skills-right-assessing-and-anticipating-changing-skill-needs_9789264252073-en#page3

Today, the unions can still turn out a mass protest that brings both their members and supporters into the streets, giving a sense of strength. But at least some of it is illusory; rarely do strikes shut down the country entirely—rather, they inconvenience it.

Although unions retain a special significance here, especially to left-leaning political parties, their heyday in France has passed, labor experts say and union leaders, in their more candid moments, concede."[172]

Talking of global talent pools, the ADP Research Institute, a specialized group within ADP, conducted a qualitative and quantitative study among employers and employees in four major regions: North America, Europe, Latin America, and Asia-Pacific. The study surveyed employers and employees based on five basic human needs: freedom, knowledge, stability, self-management, and meaning. One of its main findings was that there are divergent expectations across different regions:

"U.S. respondents were excited about the prospect of technology supplementing some of their workload, while Canadians expressed concern that this trend would threaten their job security. U.S. workers expressed resistance to a future lack of workplace hierarchy, but Canadians were hopeful about this shift. European workers claimed that a shift toward self-management is already underway in their workplaces, but they were skeptical regarding the elimination of hierarchy. In Latin America, there was a lack of belief that workplaces would do away with hierarchies and move toward increased self-management. Surprisingly, Asia-Pacific workers' responses reflected a belief that gravitation toward self-management and a dissolving of company hierarchy would happen in the future. This change would be particularly

---

[172] http://www.nytimes.com/2016/05/28/world/europe/france-unions.html?_r=0

revolutionary in this region where company structure has traditionally been a strong cultural characteristic."[173]

Who's to Blame?

It's easy to blame corporations, the government, politicians, unions, or the education system for the confusing labor market.

Part of the blame has to start at home. We are all parents who outsource education to schools. According to the most recent National Survey of Science and Mathematics Education, conducted in 2012, 58% of elementary math classes had access to calculators, but only 13% used them at least once a week. A similar disparity existed at the middle-school level, where 77% of math classes had access to calculators, but only 40% used them weekly.[174] There is no reason why parents should not rectify this at home.

At the other extreme are "helicopter parents," who meddle too much with education and overly pressure their children. There is a certain family pride and social status associated with a higher degree. The reality is that the acquaintances you make in those schools often pay off more than the actual education.

Ellison of Oracle, in his USC commencement speech first described in Chapter 1, summarized the conflict that many young people face when it comes to parental and peer pressure:

> "This was a pivotal moment in my life. My family was still mad at me for not going to medical school and now my wife was divorcing me because I lacked ambition. It looked like a reoccurrence of the same old problem. Once again I was unable to live up to the expectations of others. But this time I was not disappointed in myself for failing to be the person

[173] http://www.adp.com/tools-and-resources/adp-research-institute/insights/insight-item-detail.aspx?id=627B8AA8-3DA0-41FB-86CD-9FD9B583A157&CID=iP_SOC_TWT_All_PaidSOC_Link_ADPRI_Mobile_EvolutionWork_V14_Jan_16
[174] http://www.wsj.com/articles/calculators-in-class-use-them-or-lose-them-1463756482

they thought I should be. Their dreams and my dreams were different. I would never confuse the two of them again."

Economic data continues to show advanced degrees result in higher lifetime earnings. Little of that data, however, factors the "investment" in foregone income and the shockingly expensive cost of advanced education.

We are operating in a chaotic labor economy with all kinds of confusing signals. That means we are making decisions about automation in less-than-optimal conditions. The following chapter outlines some guiding principles to consider from three points of view—societal, enterprise, and personal.

CHAPTER 11

Thriving in the Silicon Collar Economy: Policy Perspectives

∿➤

In the course of writing this book, I had a chance to think long and hard about President John F. Kennedy's famous quote: "Ask not what your country can do for you, ask what you can do for your country." What is the role of government in this changing man/machine equilibrium, and what, in turn, should our corporate and individual responsibilities be?

A Societal Perspective

First, here are some thoughts on government policy as we worry about "jobless futures."

In the year 2000 GE Annual Report, then-CEO Jack Welch had a remarkable section titled "Relishing Change" which quoted:

> "We've long believed that when the rate of change inside an institution becomes slower than the rate of change outside, the end is in sight. The only question is when."[175]

---

[175] http://www.ge.com/annual00/download/images/GEannual00.pdf

As I was writing this book, I was repeatedly reminded that many of the problems with the job economy are the result of not everyone playing by the same "clock". It's as if some of us are ruled by the basketball 24-second shot clock, and others by the minutes and hours on their chess timers.

Corporations are leading shorter lives and have moved away from lifetime employment and pensions. But corporate HR groups—who only source a small fraction of their talent needs in a world of outsourcing and franchising—still insist on over-qualified employees, and thus create "credential inflation." They put candidates through 10–15 interviews and months of agony.

Workers, themselves, have moved to shorter tenures—the average American worker is said to rotate through seven jobs in his or her career. Economic data continues to show advanced degrees result in higher lifetime earnings. The data, however, does not factor the significant cost of this advanced education and income foregone during that time, or the fact that some workers spend longer at school than they will at any single job in their careers.

We complain about jobless growth, yet most countries report millions of unfilled positions. Unions continue with the only tool—strikes—they appear to have in their arsenal, even as they acknowledge those work slowdowns are perceived as a nuisance and hurts their image even more. Many workers have embraced the "gig economy" but find few portable benefits or a safety net for their lifestyles. Government data on the changing labor market is outdated. The next revision to the Standard Occupational Classification (SOC) system is due in 2018, eight years after the last one. Plans call for later versions to be revised once a decade.

A different time-clock issue is showing up in the EU. In the U.S., people are mobile. It is estimated that one in 40 Americans moves across state lines every year. In Europe, it is much, much slower, maybe 1 in 400. East Europeans are changing that dynamic, but the Brexit vote was partly about too much mobility across borders (interestingly, the English are some of the most mobile in the European community). More recently, there has also been a flood of refugees into the EU. It's too much change and too fast.

So, we have a social policy issue—how do we get different constituents to align their clocks so as to not keep gumming up the labor economy?

Universal Basic Income?

The pessimism around automation and jobless futures is leading to serious discussions on the "Universal Basic Income"—a no-strings-attached payment to each citizen whether they work or don't work.

Futurism reported in early 2016:

> "On March 30th, Kela—Finland's Social Insurance Institution—released a preliminary report on universal basic income. The group recommended a two-year pilot that would distribute a 550-euro monthly wage to 10,000 working adults. The Finnish government will vote on the proposal this month. On March 11th, the Swiss Ministry of Social Security revealed that it would cost just $25 billion to provide a UBI to the country. On June 5th, the Swiss government will vote on a referendum that could give citizens as much as 2,500 francs ($2,623) per month. Four cities in The Netherlands are planning UBI experiments for 2016. Utrecth's 'See What Works' program would conduct an experiment that would give citizens $980. One group would receive it unconditionally, while others will be required to volunteer—or not work at all."[176]

Switzerland has since had its referendum and rejected the UBI, but many believe it will likely get adopted in some form during the next few years. *New Scientist* reported:

---

[176] http://futurism.com/images/universal-basic-income-answer-automation/

"However, basic-income campaigners were celebrating that evening, saying their objective was to get people talking. The conversation continues. Maybe the mark of ultimate success for the proponents of universal income, says Hoeijmakers, will be if at parties the unfashionable question 'what do you do?' morphs into: 'why do you do?'"[177]

In the UK, the Royal Society for the encouragement of Arts, Manufactures and Commerce (RSA) has been thinking about several aspects of what it refers to as Basic Income:

"To assess viability, we set out a series of tests. The first is a moral test. In other words, does Basic Income correspond with widely held moral precepts? Secondly, is Basic Income achievable within the parameters of the current system of tax, ie could it be fiscally neutral or near neutral? Thirdly, are distributional consequences of a Basic Income especially for the least well-off acceptable politically and in terms of justice? Finally, would Basic Income underpin widespread creativity when compared to current institutions?"[178]

You could dismiss these concepts as European socialist thinking. But how do you explain a venture capital firm, the Y Combinator, trying out a UBI trial on its own in the U.S.?

"We'd like to fund a study on basic income—i.e., giving people enough money to live on with no strings attached. I've been intrigued by the idea for a while, and although there's been a lot of discussion, there's fairly little data about how it would work. It's true that we have systems in place to give people resources, but the bureaucracy and qualification

---

[177] https://www.newscientist.com/article/mg23030791-100-what-happens-if-we-pay-everyone-just-to-live/
[178] https://medium.com/@thersa/creative-citizen-creative-state-a3cef3f25775#. p6jtfuu9l

requirements make it a very imperfect approximation of what most people mean when talking about a basic income. We have some examples of something close to a basic income in other countries, but we'd like to see how it would work in the US. I think it's good to start studying this early. I'm fairly confident that at some point in the future, as technology continues to eliminate traditional jobs and massive new wealth gets created, we're going to see some version of this at a national scale."[179]

Fans of UBI cite the example of Harper Lee:

> "One Christmas in the late fifties, a generous friend gave her a year's wages as a gift with the note, 'You have one year off from your job to write whatever you please. Merry Christmas.'"[180]

A year later, Lee had produced a draft of *To Kill a Mockingbird*. Published two years later, it won the Pulitzer Prize for Fiction, sold 30 million copies, and won such polls as "Best novel of the century."[181]

Forget that Lee or J.K. Rowling or Tom Clancy are one-in-a-million successes in a highly fragmented book market. Or that we should all earn our own such guardian angels, not count on our government to be one.

What's concerning is the urgency of those proposing UBI—they are presuming automation will have its dire impact in the near future. As we have seen throughout this book, automation takes years, if not decades, to impact occupations. It displaces specific tasks, not complete jobs. Technologies always seem to meander and many end up with unintended, often positive consequences.

---

[179] https://blog.ycombinator.com/basic-income
[180] http://priceonomics.com/the-basic-income-guarantee/
[181] http://priceonomics.com/the-basic-income-guarantee/

Warren Buffett, the (fairly liberal) tycoon proposes something different—a restructured Earned Income Tax Credit (EITC), "which currently goes to millions of low-income workers. Payments to eligible workers diminish as their earnings increase. But there is no disincentive effect: A gain in wages always produces a gain in overall income. The process is simple: You file a tax return, and the government sends you a check. In essence, the EITC rewards work and provides an incentive for workers to improve their skills. Equally important, it does not distort market forces, thereby maximizing employment. The existing EITC needs much improvement. Fraud is a big problem; penalties for it should be stiffened. There should be widespread publicity that workers can receive free and convenient filing help. An annual payment is now the rule; monthly installments would make more sense, since they would discourage people from taking out loans while waiting for their refunds to come through. Dollar amounts should be increased, particularly for those earning the least."[182]

Not so fast, say people like Silvia Avram at the University of Essex, UK. "She recently asked people to perform a tedious task to earn money under different taxation models. The participants were divided into two groups. One group started with a lump sum that was reduced as they earned—much as would happen under a negative income tax—while the others were taxed as they earned. Both groups ended up with the same money for a given amount of work, but the first group was far quicker to quit the task, suggesting that a well-documented human tendency to loss aversion was kicking in: we are wired to place more importance on minimising losses on what we already have than realising gains of the same value."[183]

So, here is another set of policy questions to ponder: UBI or credits? Or should we use any funds set aside for either model to invest instead in rapid retraining programs that allow workers

---

[182] http://www.wsj.com/articles/better-than-raising-the-minimum-wage-1432249927
[183] https://www.newscientist.com/article/mg23030791-100-what-happens-if-we-pay-everyone-just-to-live/

to transition to new skills to adjust to the previously discussed 24-second shot clock? How about investment in energy, health, and road infrastructure which will generate a new generation of jobs?

The Ethics of Technology

We introduced in Chapter 5 the observation that even with machines growing in capability, thorny ethical issues are being swept under the rug. It's about to get worse, far worse. Think of the far reaching consequences of the genome editing technique, CRISPR-Cas9. "Just four years old, this discovery is transforming research into how to treat disease, what we eat and how we'll generate electricity, fuel our cars and even save endangered species. Experts believe that CRISPR can be used to reprogram the cells not just in humans but also in plants, insects—practically any piece of DNA on the planet."[184]

Or the robot designed to challenge Asimov's first law about robots not hurting humans. "Alexander Reben, a roboticist and artist, has built a tabletop robot whose sole mechanical purpose is to hurt people. The harm caused by Reben's robot is nothing more than a pinprick, albeit one delivered at high speed, causing the maximum amount of pain a small needle can inflict on a fingertip. And interestingly, he designed the machine so that injury is inflicted randomly. Sometimes the robot strikes. Sometimes it doesn't. Even Reben, when he exposes his fingertip to danger, has no idea if he'll end up shedding blood or not." Reben's stated goal: "I wanted to make a robot that does this that actually exists . . . That was important, to take it out of the thought experiment realm into reality, because once something exists in the world, you have to confront it. It becomes more urgent. You can't just pontificate about it."[185]

Google and Oxford University researchers have outlined, in an academic paper, thoughts around a "kill switch"—"how future

---

[184] http://time.com/4379503/crispr-scientists-edit-dna/
[185] http://www.fastcompany.com/3059484/mind-and-machine/this-robot-intentionally-hurts-people-and-makes-them-bleed

intelligent machines could be coded to prevent them from learning to over-ride human input."[186]

These are all signs that society needs to start addressing
many of the ethical issues raised by increased automation, like
what should an autonomous car target, if an accident is unavoid-
able? What to do about shopping bots that are programmed to
anonymously buy illegal merchandise on the Dark Web? What
to do about drone warfare that, while supposedly surgical, is
also dispassionate compared to hand-to-hand combat? How to
prevent algorithms from taking on biases—if a system is trained
on photos of overwhelmingly white people, how will it deal with
nonwhite faces?

In *The New Polymath:* I quoted Prof. Herman Tavani, who
teaches ethics at Rivier College,

> "There are purists who will argue the way we should look
> at ethical issues today has not changed since the days of
> Plato and his views in The Republic like those on censor-
> ship. On the other hand, some assume that every new
> technology introduces new ethical issues. For example,
> some suggest that recent encryption technologies generate
> brand-new ethical issues, such as new privacy issues that
> could not have existed before the introduction of encryp-
> tion technology.
>
> I am somewhere in between. As existing technologies
> continue to mature and evolve, many of the ethical issues
> associated with them are basically variations of existing
> ethical problems that introduce themselves in new ways.
> At bottom, these issues are still about dignity, respect, fair-
> ness, obligations to assist others in need, and so forth. But
> the rate of change has increased significantly, as well as the
> scope and scale affecting these issues, so we cannot infer

---

[186] http://www.bbc.com/news/technology-36472140

that cybertechnology has not raised some special issues for ethics."

And that was six years ago.

As a society, should we not have a framework to surface and debate these ethical issues?

Notice that I am posing questions for these societal and governmental matters. I am not arrogant enough to suggest I have many answers. I raise them because they merit vigorous discussion. I am a bit more specific when it comes to enterprise and personal perspectives. Let's look next at enterprise considerations when it comes to automation decisions.

An Enterprise Perspective

Most enterprises have structured processes for making technology decisions. They know how to define their requirements, draft vendor RFPs, develop business cases, etc. It would appear that automation decisions could easily follow such processes.

However, as we have seen in the early sections, the decisions are much more complex than just defining specs and budgets for drones and cognitive bots. The decisions are also increasingly being made in ethically and even politically charged environments.

We need to look at additional considerations that enterprises need to factor. I call this the C List because these are not the foremost issues on decision-makers' minds but still definitely should be taken into account:

- Conversations
- Customers
- Change
- Competence

Conversations

Marc Benioff, founder and CEO of Salesforce, has commented that there is a "third [political] party emerging in this country, which is the party of CEOs"[187] He is talking about activist CEOs who are confronting politicians in public ways not seen in the past.

GE CEO Jeff Immelt felt compelled to write an op-ed in response to Democratic candidate Bernie Sanders' comments that GE is among the companies that are supposedly "destroying the moral fabric" of America due to purported corporate greed and outsourcing jobs:

> "The senator has never bothered to stop by our aviation plant in Rutland, Vt. We've been investing heavily (some $100 million in recent years), hiring and turning out some of the world's finest jet-engine components in Vermont since the 1950s. The plant employs more than 1,000 people who are very good at what they do. It's a picture of first-rate jobs with high wages, advanced manufacturing in a vital industry—how things look when American workers are competing and winning—and Vermont's junior senator is always welcome to come by for a tour."[188]

Tim Cook, CEO of Apple, did not directly address the candidate from the right, Donald Trump, and his call for a boycott of his company's products if it did not move manufacturing back to the U.S., but he did tell *Time*:

> "We understand Congress sets laws. But we [see] it as our role not to just let it happen. I mean too many times in history has this happened, where the government overreached, did something that in retrospect somebody should have stood up and said 'Stop.' We see that this is our moment to stand up and say 'Stop.' And force a dialogue. And that dialogue

---

[187] http://money.cnn.com/2015/04/01/news/salesforce-benioff-indiana-religious-freedom-law/

[188] https://www.washingtonpost.com/opinions/ge-ceo-bernie-sanders-says-were-destroying-the-moral-fabric-of-america-hes-wrong/2016/04/06/8499bc8c-fc23-11e5-80e4-c381214de1a3_story.html

may, I don't know how it'll go. I'm optimistic. But I don't know at the end of the day. But I see that as our role."[189]

Lord John Browne, former CEO of BP, wrote in an op-ed:

"The U.K. rightly prides itself on punching above its weight in world affairs. We occupy an enviable role in the world. Those campaigning for Brexit either do not understand or do not care that the U.K.'s global power, which is substantial, is enlarged by EU membership."[190]

diginomica reported, just prior to the UK Brexit vote:

"34 UK-based tech CEOs—including heads of country or region of US global operations—have made the strongest statement to date, arguing that Brexit could stall the UK's tech growth engine. The signatories include the UK heads of Microsoft, Hewlett Packard Enterprise, CSC, IBM and SAP as well as indigenous UK firms such as Skyscape and BT."[191]

The problem is that the person on the street does not read these columns. They are more likely to listen to politicians and Google for a CEO's compensation and focus on inequality issues. They can find all kinds of negative stories about suicides at Foxconn-run Apple plants. None of those stories analyze the seasonal migrations of labor in China, the family pressures from China's "one child policy," and the peer competition young workers face. It is so much easier to blame Apple. It's the same with BP. Among thousands of stories about the Deepwater Horizon spill, one will

---

[189] http://time.com/4261796/tim-cook-transcript/
[190] http://www.wsj.com/articles/a-vote-to-leave-europe-means-a-lesser-britain-1466374424
[191] http://diginomica.com/2016/06/20/london-technology-week-uk-tech-leaders-take-a-stand-on-brexit/

find very little about BP's investment in safety in its refineries, pipelines, and rigs.

Business interests are being targeted quite often and not just by hostile politicians. The *Harvard Business Review* wrote about Big Business and its role in the context of an angry populace:

> "There is an even subtler harm in capital-allocation decisions when companies hoard $1.9 trillion in cash, hold foreign profits overseas, and use their capital to buy back stock. Escalating wealth driven by a bull market cannot be divorced from the atrophying of the middle class when stock repurchases and cash reserves nudge earnings per share and stock prices higher but do nothing to create employment or increase national productivity. Given that the wealthiest 10% of Americans own 81% of all stocks and mutual funds, these uses of corporate cash are a direct transfer of corporate profits away from creating jobs and capital investment, increasing income inequality."[192]

Given the scrutiny corporations are likely to attract about automation and job-related matters, I hope they take into consideration this book's arguments and combat the emotional, pessimistic views about job losses in the market. Also, they will be much more persuasive if they are more transparent about their employment decision-making process than they have been in the past. Like Immelt above, CEOs should be proactively talking about and showcasing their workers and workplaces. Don't use the glib "people are our most important asset" talk—showcase exemplary workers with the machines that allow them to excel.

Customers

It is healthy to look at automation using a customer lens. Would customers want a process automated if it removed inefficiencies?

---

[192] https://hbr.org/2016/03/how-big-business-created-the-politics-of-anger

Or would they prefer the human contact to continue? Business customers can also provide input on internal processes, especially if there are quantifiable savings.

As we saw in Chapter 1, Avi Haksar at the Rosewood Sand Hill discussed how his guests expect high touch, whereas those at midpriced business hotels are moving to mobile guest check-in, robotic butlers, and other automation. As we also saw in Chapter 8, customers in many settings are ambivalent about self-service, especially if no savings are being passed along. That should be a litmus test—are we willing to pass along any savings from the automation to customers?

In Chapter 1 we introduced Amazon Web Services (AWS). AWS is a clear benchmark to emulate when it comes to passing along savings from automation. It says it has delivered 51 price cuts over a decade around data center services.[193] You can nitpick the details of Amazon's claim but, in comparison, outsourcers like IBM and HPE lock customers into multiyear contracts with hardly any price cuts for that tenure. Customers have rewarded AWS for its high level of automation and for the beneficial economics. When it comes to cloud infrastructure, AWS has more market share than that of its top competitors—Microsoft, IBM, Google, Oracle, and HPE—all put together, and it is on a $10 billion revenue run rate. Watch out accounting and outsourcing firms—customers would similarly like more automation in your processes, but only if you can pass along related savings.

Change
Most technology projects have learned to factor in a change-management element. With automation projects, there are two additional wrinkles. The first is that technology change is continuous. As we saw around AI, it has been evolving since the 1950s, and robotics since even earlier. Like an airline, you need to plan

---

[193] https://aws.amazon.com/blogs/aws/happy-new-year-ec2-price-reduction-c4-m4-and-r3-instances/

for a 20–30 year horizon for the fleet, with significant upgrades every few years. An example of such rapid, ongoing change comes from the test automation space that every IT department is familiar with:

> "SQA was acquired by Rational Software which in turn was acquired by IBM. Newer versions of the toolset are still branded as Rational. Mercury was acquired by Hewlett-Packard and the updated toolset rebranded under the wider HP logo. Segue branded their toolset under the Silk banner and although the company was acquired by Borland which was in turn acquired by MicroFocus, the toolset and its descendants are still branded as Silk."[194]

And just when that dust appeared to have settled:

> "During his opening keynote address at the Google Test Automation Conference 2011, entitled 'Test is Dead,' Alberto Savoia states that (traditional) software testing is dead or on the decline. He suggests that (start-up) companies are putting less emphasis on testing and more emphasis on releasing software quickly and continuously."[195]

Additionally, as Dr. Michael Blum pointed out in Chapter 1, technology implementations often lead to a "productivity paradox" wherein the worker/technology combination can lead to lowered efficiency. In Chapter 8, Mary Lacity and Leslie Willcocks identified "systemantics"—quirks and shortcomings that are just as endemic to systems as their strengths.

The second wrinkle concerns the change in the nature of jobs and the skill sets needed for them. In Chapter 1, Josh Tetrick mentioned how his R&D labs require the skills of plant biologists,

---

[194] https://www.linkedin.com/pulse/20141007123253-16089094-a-very-brief-history-of-test-automation
[195] http://www.testingreferences.com/testinghistory.php

molecular biologists, biochemists, process engineers (including certification experts), data scientists, and computational biologists— among others. We heard Brian Sommer describe in Chapter 7 how accounting departments of the future may need to include skills around statistics, data science, analytics, algorithms, and social sciences.

Competence

An accountant, a lawyer, and an automation engineer are led to the guillotine, having been convicted of grievous crimes. The accountant is first in line, but the falling blade jams halfway down. The executioner tells him, "You may be unethical but my professional ethics require me to spare your life." The lawyer is second in line, and again the falling blade sticks and the man is spared. Finally, the automation engineer is walked up, and he confidently addresses the executioner, "I know what your problem is. It's the actuator."

With today's automation, it is highly unlikely any single engineer could be that specific. You also hope he is less exuberant. As we have seen throughout this book, different robots, drones, and algorithms can handle specific tasks. Contract manufacturers and systems integrators may need to work together to develop customized machines. Similarly, on the customer side, process and automation engineers may need to collaborate closely.

Most enterprises have a poor track record even on well-trodden technology projects. Automation calls for an even more realistic assessment of project success.

Finally, let's look at personal manifestos when it comes to the changing labor economy.

The Personal Manifesto

Most of us grew up reading Richard Scarry's illustrated books where anthropomorphic animals went about their daily lives in Busytown. One of his most popular books, *What Do People Do All*

Day? showed these characters like Grocer Cat at work. The *New Yorker* called it "Positively guaranteed to please any small child."

For eons, many of us have derived our self-esteem from our work lives. In fact, many of us continue with names which reflect the trades of our ancestors. It could be the Chinese Chong (derived from bow maker), the English Weaver, the Egyptian El-Mofti (from Arabic for legal expert), German Baumgartner (related to orchard), or the Indian Bhattacharya (from Sanskrit for teacher)—and there are thousands of other names derived from occupations in various societies.

If Scarry were to write the book today, he would have many more occupations to portray. And today, Farmer Alfafa could easily become Captain Salty over the course of his life. We have so much choice.

Don Henley, the singer and drummer of the immensely popular band, the Eagles, described in a Netflix documentary[196] how the group broke up for 14 years, and their fears when they decided to reunite. Would the band jell after the acrimonious breakup? Would audiences still relate to their genre of music? Upon breakup, Henley had famously announced they would come together "when Hell freezes over." The reunion tour and several since managed to pack even larger arenas than the Eagles did at the height of their earlier popularity.

Henley later told *Rolling Stone* magazine:

> "And another rare thing that happened to us, that I mention in the documentary, is we were fortunate enough to have one of the rarest of things in American life, which is a second act."[197]

---

[196] http://dvd.netflix.com/Movie/History-of-the-Eagles/70267553
[197] http://www.rollingstone.com/music/news/q-a-don-henley-opens-up-about-the-history-of-the-eagles-at-sundance-20130120#ixzz4CKVylvqY

Few of us can aspire to the kind of blowout second act Henley talks about, but everyone of us can plan on more modest second and later acts in our careers.

It's actually easier than it sounds. Never before in history have we had so many career choices. As we saw in Chapter 10, The Bureau of Labor Statistics classifies workers into one of 840 detailed occupations, in accordance with the 2010 Standard Occupational Classification (SOC) system. CareerPlanners.com does an even more granular listing of job descriptions, and lists 12,000 separate jobs.[198]

The 2018 SOC will likely grow the number of occupations, just like the 2010 version had over the previous year 2000 version. The 2010 version had significant updates to information technology, health care, and human resource occupations,[199] and given the growing influence of STEM in our economy, the 2018 one should have similar significant updates.

We are also not staying long in our jobs. Anecdotally, you hear the average American holds seven jobs in their careers. According to the BLS, the average person born in the latter years of the baby boom (1957–1964) held 11.7 jobs from age 18 to age 48, and nearly half of these jobs were held from ages 18 to 24.[200] While many think the BLS data is skewed, it is at least partially corroborated by Census data. The typical American worker's tenure with his or her current employer was 3.8 years in 1996, 3.5 years in 2000, and 4.1 years in 2008.[201]

And the BLS barely scratches "nontraditional employment scenarios." A blog post on LinkedIn describes three such scenarios to consider when creating a professional social media profile:

1. You are working more than one job.

---

[198] http://www.careerplanner.com/DOTindex.cfm
[199] http://www.bls.gov/soc/FRn_May_22_2014.pdf
[200] http://www.bls.gov/news.release/nlsoy.nr0.htm
[201] http://www.wsj.com/articles/SB10001424052748704206804575468162805877990

2. You've been working for yourself and now you want a full-time job.
3. You've been out of the workforce for several years and want to get back in the game.[202]

The three scenarios, in turn, describe a multitude of employment profiles these days. Let's take the first scenario about working more than one job. Many Uber drivers often have a different day job, as we saw in Chapter 4. Working for yourself could mean founding a start-up, investing in a franchise, or working as an independent contractor. Look around—see relatively new jobs—alternative medicine practitioners, ethnic restaurants, eBay businesses, day traders, adventure travel guides. Being out of the workforce is not just a euphemism for being unemployed—you could be caring for young kids or you could be taking a "gap year", as many young workers do and travel the world.

This is the new normal, and yet there is so much emotion around layoffs at "greedy companies," and in reverse, corporations complain about "disloyal" employees who "jump around" even as we saw earlier, a vast majority are not directly employed by the corporations.

The reality is that we are all getting our chances at second, third, and even later acts. Instead of getting angry and upset at corporations, politicians, or each other, we should stay agile and keep following the money. I realize this is easier advice for younger workers but this book is full of examples of second and third acts. Brian Sommer used to be an Accenture partner; now he has a successful analyst and advisory business. Curtis Beebe was a technology consultant; now he operates three restaurants. Nina Kohli-Laven has worked in a wide range of jobs spanning the world in her young career. Dennis Howlett was a Chartered Accountant, then a journalist, and now he runs a successful media property. Dr. Russell Fricano was a planner in Los Angeles; now

---

[202] https://blog.linkedin.com/2011/08/30/profile-tips

he is in academia. Then there is the unbelievable example of James Tadae Shimoura.

Let me add from my own personal experience. My blogging career started a decade ago and I have logged over 10,000 posts. My book writing career did not start till six years ago, and since then I have averaged a book a year. Before that, I was a PwC technology consultant, a Gartner market analyst, a start-up entrepreneur (it failed), a speaker, and an adviser to CIOs. Wait, many of those still continue as my jobs.

I agonized for months before I left PwC in 1995. I had a young family and many told me I was stupid to walk away from a long-term career. Looking back I am glad I made the move. If you can find lifetime employment, earn plates for 25 years of service, and qualify for a pension, enjoy your good fortune. The rest of us need to stay nimble and plan on constantly learning new skills. And making new machine friends.

The good news is there is plenty of work to go around for all for us. The IRS reported in 2013 that the total Adjusted Gross Income Americans reported on our tax returns was over $9 trillion.[203] That's after adjustments, so actual income is likely another 20% higher. The majority of that income comes from wages and small business income. Many economies around the world offer their citizens similar opportunities.

How can I be so optimistic about people's ability to find a niche for themselves?

Look around your neighborhood. In mine, I see so many individuals who have found successful ways to generate a living, most without advanced degrees. At Coco Cuts, Blanca has tidied my hair for 25 years. She still calls me "Binny," and over the years has kept me informed on my hair loss. There is Lee, who for the same number of years has been repairing and polishing our shoes. We talk about his native South Korea and the supply chain for his materials. His shop is very popular, and if you think

---

[203] https://www.irs.gov/uac/soi-tax-stats-whats-new-in-the-individual-area

you work hard, you ought to see Lee, whom I have never seen relax, as he works while talking to his customers. There's Tender Touch Cleaners which has dry cleaned our clothes for just as long. Our local seamstress at Hyons Alterations is in such demand that you have to wait at least a week to get the work done. Our former nanny, Linda, is still looking after young children, and has a waiting list. Ditto with Mel, the dog sitter on our street.

My wife is a regular visitor to Barnes & Noble, and she tells me that during the week, after school hours, the tables are full of educators working with children on their school work. We used to have Dan come to our house and work with the children on their math problems. He now has an online service which offers tutoring and test prep services, a significant expansion of his reach.

Then there are home-related services. Chet's monitors the house for termites; Calico fine-tunes our air conditioning. The pool is serviced by Pool Masters, a small company run by a couple who both have business degrees but find they like the outdoor life better than working in an office.

When it comes to dining, we have favorite restaurants like Cafe de Siam for Thai cooking, and Mandy's for the Cuban experience. They keep multiple family members employed. It is worth noting that many excellent waiters, waitresses, and bar staff in our area earn far more money in a year than school teachers, and do not need college degrees.

None of these businesses will ever need to hire Goldman Sachs, but they represent a wide range of skills that lets them smile and serve. They have survived and thrived for decades.

Which is why I relate to billionaire Warren Buffett as he pointed out in his annual investor letter in early 2016:

> "American GDP per capita is now about $56,000. As I mentioned last year that—in real terms—is a staggering six times the amount in 1930, the year I was born, a leap far beyond the wildest dreams of my parents or their contemporaries. U.S. citizens are not intrinsically more intelligent today, nor

do they work harder than did Americans in 1930. Rather, they work far more efficiently and thereby produce far more. This all-powerful trend is certain to continue: America's economic magic remains alive and well."

and

"It's an election year, and candidates can't stop speaking about our country's problems (which, of course, only they can solve). As a result of this negative drumbeat, many Americans now believe that their children will not live as well as they themselves do. That view is dead wrong: The babies being born in America today are the luckiest crop in history."[204]

Feel the need to be an activist? Don't just vent on talk shows or blogs. Call your Congressman and lobby for portable benefits. Push for a safety net for individuals who do multiple jobs. If they are thinking of funding Universal Basic Income, ask them to also consider using some of the funds instead for rapid retraining programs to allow workers to transition to new skills. Or to invest in the energy, health, and road infrastructure that will generate a new generation of jobs.

Forget about trade unions and strikes. If you want corporations to respect you, leverage your purchasing, not your muscle or brainpower. Yell at AAA and AARP to negotiate better discounts for individuals. They get piddling discounts on travel and insurance for the purchasing power their members represent. Support the Consumer Reports Foundation—they are one of the few entities which unabashedly looks out for purchasing leverage for the small guy.

Salute your fellow exemplary human workers and emulate them. In this book, we have discussed several standout examples:

---

[204] http://www.berkshirehathaway.com/letters/2015ltr.pdf

Mumbai dabbawalas with their Six Sigma delivery record. UPS employees with millions of miles of accident-free driving. Foxconn employees who have delivered billions of high-quality Apple devices under incredible time constraints. Amazon data center employees who have delivered over 50 price cuts over the last decade.

And rejoice that humans still want the human touch. RoboGames, an annual event, pits robotic athletes against each other. Their coaches are human engineers. As its organizer admits, even in its 12th year, it is on a shoestring budget.[205] Human athletes draw dramatically bigger audiences. Rock star Prince once commented, "You can't get a machine to play like my drummer." Actually, no machine could dream up the three-minute solo guitar performance Prince delivered in 2004 at the posthumous George Harrison induction into the Rock and Roll Hall of Fame. You can watch it on YouTube. You could also watch Eagles' hits on YouTube. Yet, the band continued to draw huge live audiences.

Don't cling to dull, dirty, dangerous tasks. Allow machines to to take them over. Would it not be better to move to more creative, productive tasks? Use your friendship with machines to your advantage. Remember the *Star Wars* series? The young Anakin Skywalker benefited from understanding Binary spoken by astromech droids like R2-D2. Remember *Avatar*? Jake Sully learned to use the psionic link unit to overcome his paraplegic limitations.

In comparison, working with today's machine learning or drones is both a breeze and a skill which should be widely marketable across industries.

So, to go back to Kennedy's quote—accept your personal responsibility and use it to get a full, satisfying share of Silicon Collar Nation!

---

[205] http://robogames.net/ab-history.php

The Allure of the Human Touch

⌇➤

Like many descendants of immigrants, David Sugimoto (introduced in the Prologue) yearned to learn more about his roots. Eight decades after his grandfather, James Tadae Shimora, embarked on his long journey from the small Japanese island of Shikoku to Detroit, Sugimoto reversed the journey—and did it in under a day, courtesy of a Boeing 747.

Even after a comfortable flight, Japan can be disorienting. As chef, globetrotter, and TV food host Anthony Bourdain once said, "Rigorously conventional on one hand, batshit crazy party animals on the other, Japan will always confuse outsiders looking in."[206]

Sugimoto expressed how he felt on his first trip to Japan in 1988:

> "I was born in Detroit, which had a small Japanese community. When I was in junior high school, we moved to Houston, which had a tiny Japanese community, and in high school we moved to Corpus Christi, Texas, which had none at all.
>
> So, I really did not know much about Japan as I took my first trip there when I was 33. I had just read Amy Tan's

---

[206] http://www.cnn.com/video/shows/anthony-bourdain-parts-unknown/season-2/tokyo/

book, *The Joy Luck Club*. It's a story about the daughter of Chinese immigrants who returns with her mother's ashes back to her birthplace in China. She comments that when she landed in China, and saw everyone who looked like her, a feeling overcame her that she had arrived home.

When I landed in Japan, I knew exactly what she was talking about. I saw all of these people who looked like me and I started to understand my grandparents a lot better. It was a very moving experience. I sometimes catch myself calling it my first trip 'back' to Japan. I've been back to Japan many times since then, and it's so different from anything that you ever see in America."

Sugimoto saw extremes in automation and in artisans:

"Japanese comfort with technology goes all the way back to the 1860s during the Meiji Restoration. The feudal system was supplanted by today's Japan. They saw what happened in China, in Vietnam, and other parts of Asia that were colonized. A consensus emerged that the best way to prevent being colonized was to industrialize and Westernize.

The samurai were put in charge of that. Yes, they were the warrior class, but they were also well educated and trained in managing large organizations. There was also a big artistic component to their training which included practices like the ikebana—the flower arranging—and tea ceremonies. The Mitsubishis, the Sumitomos and other big conglomerates of today are descendants of that society. The artistic component has been infused into today's corporate culture."

Japan nurtures master craftsmen—Shokunin—such as metalsmiths who recreate Samurai swords using primitive, small-lot steel with months, or even years, of flattening and rolling of the blades. There is little written documentation to guide them to recreate these masterpieces, which date back over a millennium. Then there are the intricacies of bonsai, the manicure of dwarf plants that the Japanese improvised from their Chinese origins. There are sushi chefs who demand the best sumeshi, rice seasoned with vinegar that is served at body temperature. Not just any rice, but only grain grown in the mountains, again related to temperatures at which the rice was conditioned.

Of course, for each of these artisanal masterpieces, there are mass-produced options. You can buy much more affordable katana swords made in China. Your local Ikea offers "mallsai"—s-curved tropical ficus plants. Conveyor-belt sushi uses sensors, magnets, and data to bring much more affordable seafood to the common person.

In artisan communities in Japan, skills are handed down over years, from master to apprentice. The goal is to produce disciples who improve on your craft. When you meet your master "on the other side," he would be disappointed if you had not trained your disciple to be your equal or better.

Then there is the mainstream, but legendary Japanese customer service. Shop assistants and hotel staff welcome customers with "Irasshaimase" and bow to them. They would be embarrassed if a customer saw them fiddling with a mobile device. You don't tip a Japanese server or taxi driver—they would be insulted. Some people complain the service is all rules-based—it is very difficult to get custom orders or service—but the attitude of respect for the customer is hard to find anywhere else in the world.

On the other end of that spectrum is the Japanese fascination with automation. Japan has the highest per capita number of vending machines. They don't just dispense sodas or cigarettes. You can buy panties, plants, sushi—just about anything—from these machines, any time of day or night. This is a country which has exported industrial robots for decades. Now it is pioneering all kinds of humanoid robots.

Sugimoto elaborated:

> "Japan is big on robotics and machines for a couple of reasons. It is a country with a rapidly aging population, with not enough young workers, and it is also ambivalent about immigration. They are turning to all kinds of service robots for several low-skill jobs, such as CareBots assisting the elderly.
>
> On my trips, I have noticed how their young are comfortable with technology. With vending machines everywhere, many selling alcohol, I was surprised they could trust their young to not abuse the access. Things have evolved, and on recent visits I have noticed cigarette machines have a card reader that reads either your driver's license or a 'tobacco passport' card for proof of age. The subway was automated long ago in Japan. It goes back to the demographics. Why have someone standing there handing out and punching tickets? I noticed how Tokyo lit up after dark. I remember two decades ago, there was an animation down the side of a building. It was a short animation of a male character taken from one of those woodblock prints but the quality of the movement and clarity was remarkable. I remember being amazed at prepaid cards with no need for coins for public phones. They used electronic boarding passes on their phones years before they were used in the U.S."

Sugimoto then turned to Japan's aesthetics:

> "I had a chance to visit Kanazawa on the west coast of Japan. Kanazawa along with Kyoto are two large cities which were spared bombing during the World War. There was little of strategic importance to the Allies. But back in the 1600s, it was a very rich area of Japan because it was ideal for growing rice, which was the currency of the day. The Maeda clan, which ran the area, imported a lot of artisans

from Kyoto and Edo, which was later renamed Tokyo. It was so abundant that the skills filtered farther down the social hierarchy and into other parts of Japan. Today, this is where people go to learn the old ancient crafts. Kanazawa's mission is to preserve this culture and encourage old crafts like papermaking, lacquerware, metalworking, stonecutting, and ceramics. When I first went to Kanazawa, the journey took a lot longer. Today, they have a bullet train line, the Shinkansen, that goes from Tokyo to Kanazawa in a little over two hours.

The artisan city is also comfortable with automation. Kanazawa is credited with giving us conveyor sushi. It's also a big textile town. I got to tour a plant owned by Tsudakoma. They make those big air-jet looms that manufacture textiles. The guy flipped the machine on for me to show how it weaves the fabric, and it was really remarkable. Of course, that was something that was carried down from the artisan times, because Kanazawa was known for the dyeing of fabrics. Two rivers run through the city, and fabric makers used to rinse the dye in the rivers.

Presentation is very important to the Japanese. Look at how Japanese restaurants present dishes. It's big on the aesthetics of how it looks, and that manifests itself in much of Japanese culture. The Japanese view technology as bringing precision. You stand on a platform waiting for the 2:51 train, and sure enough the train pulls into the station and the wheels lock and the clock clicks 2:51. Precision also shows in the industries that they focused on. We all know about the cars, but consumer electronics were a major export item. Consumer electronics are such miniaturized products, and you couldn't use your fingers and tweezers to craft circuit boards, so they had to end up using machines. I was recently taking a picture of an old Pioneer FX 1980 stereo receiver. In its day, it was technologically advanced, but if you look at its well-machined knobs it is also a beautiful work of art. On one of my trips, having come from a family rooted in the auto industry, I went to see the Lexus factory in Kyushu. Two things really stuck out. How few humans were on the line, and how clean it was. They didn't have that chain that I remembered from my childhood visits to auto plants. The cars actually sat on a moving platform. It looked more like a hospital than a car factory. I could quite honestly eat off the floor."

Societies evolve differently, and some are blessed with younger workforces than seen in Japan. Others, like the U.S., rely on immigration to keep their workforces vibrant. Every society, however, continues to blend traditional arts and crafts with modern production and automation. Rug weavers in Turkey, Gaelic teachers in Ireland, glass blowers in Murano, Italy, Shakespearean theater around the world, artisan wares on sites like Etsy and Novica—humans cherish the past, even as we are surrounded by a growing number of machines.

Artisans in the midst of automation—mankind has a long history of cherishing both. We will never get tired of the human touch, no matter how imperfect it may seem compared to the work of machines. More importantly, when man and machine collaborate for excellence, people line up for blocks to pay tribute.

Index